Policy

Concepts in the Social Sciences

Series Editor: Frank Parkin

Concepts in the Social Sciences

Policy

H. K. Colebatch

Open University Press
Buckingham

Open University Press
Celtic Court
22 Ballmoor
Buckingham
MK18 1XW

First Published 1998

A catalogue record of this book is available from the British Library

ISBN 0 335 19736 1 (pb)   0 335 19737 X (hb)

Typeset by Type Study, Scarborough
Printed in Great Britain by St Edmundsbury Press Ltd, Bury St Edmunds, Suffolk

*To Peta
who knows all about policy
but doesn't have the time
to write it down*

Contents

Acknowledgements

I would like to thank those who have contributed to the development of the analysis in this book, but it is so difficult to name them all. I have benefited from years of friendship and discussion with Bernard Schaffer (who first awakened my interest in policy), Robert Parker, John Power and John Ballard. Pieter Degeling and Peter Larmour have been lively sparring partners and co-authors, and I would like to thank them for their contribution to this project without implying that they agree with the outcome. I have been greatly stimulated by students and staff at Kuring-gai College, the University of Tasmania and the University of New South Wales, and would particularly like to thank Bill Birkett, Ralph Chapman, Sue Keen, Mark Lyons and Chris Walker for their help. I am indebted to Dick Scott and Jim March at Stanford, and Randall Smith and his colleagues at the School for Policy Studies at the University of Bristol, for their hospitality and encouragement. Anton Ploeg, David Thomas and Chris Walker read parts of the text in draft and gave me the benefit of their comments. But my greatest debt is to a policy practitioner, Peta Colebatch, who has for many years shared with me her enormous experience and understanding of the policy process, and who read the entire draft closely and critically and made many constructive suggestions. To her, and to all those who have helped me, my warmest thanks.

Hal K. Colebatch
Sydney

Preface

There are now so many books with 'policy' in the title that the reader is entitled to ask why another one is needed. It is certainly true that in recent years a substantial literature on policy has emerged, but it would be true to say that it tends to assume its subject matter: it talks about the content of policy – what health policy or environmental policy or industrial policy is or could be – without delving too deeply into what policy is as such, or where it comes from. This is the question to which this book is addressed: what does it mean to talk about policy? As a concept in the social sciences, what does the term denote?

But it is not only social scientists who are interested in policy: it is a concept in use by a wide range of participants in public life – public officials, elected representatives, activists, experts, journalists and others – who use the term in their attempts to shape the way public life in organized. To speak of 'heritage policy' (for instance) is not simply a neutral way of talking about something that is there, but a way of focusing attention on some things (such as the value of historic buildings) rather than others (such as the possibility of demolishing them and building a tower block of offices). So in examining the concept of policy, we need to take account of how it is used by practitioners as well as by academic observers.

This book is written for both the practitioner and the observer, and is addressed to a range of readers. There are those who are interested in a particular field (like the environment) and want to know what it means to have 'environmental policy', and how it is produced. There are students of the political process, who want to know how 'policy' (or 'public policy') relates to well-established analytical terms like 'politics', 'rule-making' or 'decision'. And then there are those who are interested in the broader question of the way in which we are governed, which seems to mean more than just 'what the government decides to do', but to be concerned with the way that diverse activities by different bodies are drawn together into stable and predictable patterns of action which (as often as not) come to be labelled 'policy'.

So it is seen as a 'generic' guide to policy as such, rather than an introduction to any specific sort of policy. Policy is encountered in a wide range of contexts – different fields of action, different political systems and cultures, different times and circumstances – and it would be impossible to cover them all. When I have given examples, they are usually fictitious ones, constructed to make sense to readers from as wide a range of backgrounds and experiences as possible. This is a set of questions about policy rather than a set of answers.

The Idea of Policy

Marrickville Council has approved a brothel on Marrickville Road despite concerns from some councillors [that] the brothel is located 40m from St Clement's Anglican Church . . .
    Several councillors claimed it was council's policy to consider a brothel's proximity to a church when deciding an application . . .
    At the meeting, Mayor Barry Cotter said the council had no policy to stop the brothel operating . . .
    He said if council refused the application it would be throwing away $15,000 of ratepayers' money in a court case doomed to fail.

(*The Glebe* [Sydney] 26 February 1997)

Policy is a concept which dominates our understanding of the ways we are governed. It appears that a party leader facing an impending election must have a clearly stated policy on all matters of significance. Both practitioners and observers of the political process share this concern with the central importance of policy, which is perhaps why there is so little interest in what the term means. In current political practice, it means 'a prior statement of the actions and commitments of a future government in respect of some area of activity' – their education policy, or their environment policy, or their industry policy.

It seems to operate prospectively rather than retrospectively: there is a great deal of interest in what politicians say that they are going to do, but much less interest in whether they do it. There may be a little press interest, but it is likely to appear as a background article in the weekend papers rather than on the front page. It is less common for it to be asked whether it is realistic to depict the experience of government over the last four years as the realization (or non-realization) of previously stated intentions. There seems to be more interest in the existence of policies than there is in their significance. This widespread acceptance of the term reflects the extent of the taken-for-granted in our understanding of the process of government: it is seen as a way of bringing state power to bear on particular problems, and 'policy' is the outcome – the action taken by government in relation to some defined area of practice.

But 'policy' refers to more than decisions taken by political leaders.To describe something as 'policy' is to give it a special significance. To say that it is policy that all children should remain at school until the end of Year 12 is more significant than saying that it is the preference of the teachers or the parents. The impact of government on the welfare of the people is discussed as 'social policy'. Scientific knowledge is seen as the basis for policy. Experts in climate or land use or air quality organize their knowledge as an agenda of concern for government: a contribution to the making of 'environmental policy'. The term implies something broader than simply 'what the government wants to do'. The message in an article title, 'Is there a national policy for children and youth with serious emotional disturbance?' (Koyanagi 1994) is clear: there should be a systematic pattern of activity addressed to this problem.

At the same time, the term seems to have a small-scale application, as can be seen when officials describe routine practice as 'policy' – e.g. when a clerk says, 'I can't deal with this matter over the phone: departmental policy is that all complaints must be in writing'. Here, the term is being used to protect the clerk from having to justify his or her action: I am not interested in the case that you can make, and in fact I'm not really making a choice; I'm simply following policy.

We can see already that the term can mean quite different things. Consider the following statements:

• 'The participation of women in the work force on an equal basis with men is the policy of this government.'
• 'Our policy in relation to young people and drug use is in total confusion.'
• 'Departmental policy is that students will only be given an extension for an essay if they produce a medical certificate.'

The first quotation is a statement about the values and aspirations of the government as a whole. The second probably indicates that the values and activities of various public agencies – e.g. the police, welfare authorities and the hospitals – may be inconsistent with one another. The third is a statement about the routine practice of one section of one public body. The different sorts of statement have different implications for action. For instance, the first statement quoted above might be compared to one like this:

• 'Government policy is that government contracts will only be awarded to firms which are certified by the Equal Employment Opportunity Office to be conforming to EEO guidelines.'

This is clearly a much more specific statement. It is also a statement about practice rather than a statement about goals – or to put it another way, it has its focus on process where the focus of the first statement is on outcome.

This brief discussion shows that while the term 'policy' is widely used by both academic analysts and practitioners in the field of government, it is used in a variety of ways. In this book, we will not be assuming that the term has a single, clear meaning. What is important is to clarify the way in which the term is used, and to illuminate the nature of different usages. For instance, do practitioners (who see much of their work as relating to policy – framing policy, advising on policy, negotiating changes to policy, etc.) use the term in the same way as academic observers? We want to enquire into what 'policy' means without assuming that it always has the same meaning in all contexts, and we will try to begin with a 'common-sense' understanding, and build upon it.

We can start by noting that discussion about 'policy' usually rests on three assumed characteristics of organized action – which seem natural to the participants, but which outside observers need to note and to question: *coherence*, *hierarchy* and *instrumentality*.

Coherence is the assumption that all the bits of the action fit together, that they form part of an organized whole, a single system, and policy has to do with how this system is (or should be) steered. This is something which is easier to describe in theory than to find on the ground. People involved in the process of government find that there is a wide range of people and organizations involved, with differing concerns and capacities, and varying relationships with each other and with 'the government'. For the participants, coherence is not so much one of the attributes of policy as one of the central problems: how to get all the different elements to focus on the same question in the same way. On the ground, policy-making looks less like a single-minded exercise of choice, and more like a pattern of interaction between different participants, a process of 'pulling and hauling', in which the different players try to shape activity in ways which reflect their particular perspectives.

The second assumption is *hierarchy*: that the policy process is about people at the top giving instructions. Policy is seen as authoritative determination of what will be done in some particular area, and clearly, one cannot have the various organized bodies each going its own way, whether it is the different offices of one organization, or different organizations within the broad framework of 'government'. So the policy process is concerned with the processes through which a course of action is officially endorsed. This is seen as being done by 'the government' or 'the authorities' or 'the state', but in each case, there is a sense of a central nervous system of public authority, which decides on a course of action and communicates it 'down the line'.

The third assumption is *instrumentality*: that policy is to be understood as the pursuit of particular purposes ('policy objectives'). In this perspective, public organization exists to identify and deal with problems. These problems may be fairly broadly stated ('the problem of youth unemployment') or to be more specific ('the problem of the work relevance of the senior secondary curriculum'), they may change over time and place, and the goals may be more or less clearly stated, but policy is to be understood in terms of problems and solutions.

In this view of the world, the activity of government is seen as choosing goals to solve problems, and 'policy' and 'public policy' become almost indistinguishable. Governments decide what the policy objectives are, and policy is what governments decide to do, so policy must therefore be public. The term 'public policy' also highlights the hierarchical dimension of policy: it is made by the application of public authority. But for many people, 'public policy' is too broad a term: they focus instead on the problem area to which policy is directed, and speak of 'health policy', 'transport policy', 'immigration policy', etc. These terms highlight the instrumentality of policy rather than the manner of its making, and so are not alternatives to the term 'public policy' so much as subdivisions of it.

Policy outside government

If 'policy' tends to be used to refer to what governments do, does it
have any application outside government? The departmental
policy on late essays, the church's policy on foreign investments, or
the mining company's policy on environmental protection are all
uses of the term by non-government bodies. Certainly, the term
'policy' is less common in business settings than in government.
Although the term is sometimes encountered, there is not a great
field of 'business policy' to set against 'public policy'. The direction
of business firms is more likely to be described by such terms as
'strategy' or 'corporate plans'. To some extent, steering business
firms is seen as less problematic than steering government, perhaps
reflecting the assumption that these firms have the clear purpose of
making a profit, the only question being which way they might
choose to do this, which makes statements of policy unnecessary.

Where the term 'policy' does seem to be more commonly
employed in business is in stating practice to audiences outside the
firm – e.g., 'The policy of this firm is to recruit from the local community wherever possible.' Here, the statement is, in a sense, not
only a description of practice but also a justification of it. This
would suggest that we are more likely to find business firms making
statements about their policies in areas where outsiders have an
interest: for instance, firms might state their environmental protection policy, or their policy on equal employment opportunity. They
are less likely to describe the decision to seek an export market for
a product as a policy.

In the same way, the term 'policy' is not widely used in non-
commercial non-government organizations. In a voluntary association – e.g. a community childcare centre, a church or a soccer club
– participants are reluctant to see themselves as being there to
accomplish policy objectives. The term is, however, likely to
become more common as the organization becomes more established, for reasons which are worth noting. The childcare centre, for
instance, might have started without many statements about what
its objectives were, other than 'to care for children'. But the centre
might have found it necessary to decide what to do about children
who were sick: the staff might have found that sick children could
not participate in the normal activities, and that it was difficult to
care for them without neglecting the other children. The parents of

the other children might have complained that their children were getting sick as a consequence. There might have been concerns from the public health authorities, and the centre staff might have found out that the schools had a standard response to illness, excluding children with specified ailments for prescribed periods of time. The centre might then have defined its own sickness policy, so that the staff and parents did not have to decide and negotiate each case as it came up.

We can see here that 'policy' can mean not a set of objectives for the activity, or even the guiding principles, but simply the standardization and articulation of practice: 'This is the way we do it here.' The adoption of such policies by the centre is likely to reflect a number of processes: the centre is growing and the Director wants to be sure all the staff do the same thing; increasingly, the staff have had training and want to supervise activities, not care for sick children; centre staff will become aware of practice in other centres, perhaps through an association of childcare centres; and regulatory officials may be asking increasingly specific questions about practice. In other words, articulating policy in organizations has to do with looking sideways ('Who are the relevant others, and what are they doing?') as well as with looking forwards ('Where do we want to go?').

In this example, we can see the emergence of policy within organizations seen as 'non-government'; we can also find non-government organizations being drawn into governmental policy activity. For example, the childcare centre's policy on children's illnesses and attendance would not have been developed solely within the centre. The construction of policy involves more than just government: other participants have a very significant role to play, particularly in the impact they have on which things are seen as problems and worthy of policy attention. Even if we stick to the perception that it is governments which 'make policy', it is clear that they do not make it in times and circumstances of their own choosing, and non-government is also an important part of the policy process.

The attributes of policy

'Policy' is clearly a term that is used in a variety of ways at different levels. Rather than trying to superimpose on this usage an authoritative (to us) definition of policy, it might be more fruitful to identify what it is that people are trying to label when they term something 'policy'. We can see three central elements in the ways that the term is used: authority, expertise and order.

First of all, policy rests on *authority*. To speak of something as policy implies that it has the endorsement of some authorized decision-maker. It is the authority which legitimates the policy, and policy questions flow to and from authority figures: the Minister, the General Manager, the Executive Committee. These figures may have little to do with the framing of policy, but it draws on their authority, cascading down through the organization via the principle of hierarchy.

Secondly, policy implies *expertise*. Policy is seen as a process of bringing the power of the organization to bear on some particular problem area. This implies that policy requires knowledge, both of the problem area, and of the things that might be done about it. Policy knowledge is subdivided into functional areas – education policy, transport policy, etc. – the stress being on education or transport rather than on policy. When new policy concerns appear, such as the environment or equality of opportunity in employment, they are driven initially by widely shared principles, but over time a body of specialized policy expertise is developed. And since this perspective sees policy as an exercise in skilled problem-solving, it invites the question 'Does the policy work?', which generates a further specialized field of policy evaluation.

Finally, policy is concerned with *order*. Policy implies system and consistency. The decision is not arbitrary or capricious: it is governed by a known formula of universal application. In this way, policy sets limits on the behaviour of officials; at the same time, it frees them from the need to make choices. And it draws a range of activities into a common framework: we don't just teach a foreign language to a lot of students, we have a foreign language education policy.

In this context, a major source of difficulty is the problem of consistency between different policy fields. The policy of the highways agency on building urban freeways may clash with the policy of the wildlife agency on protecting the habitat of the native fauna. The policy of the water authority to extend its supply network may be at variance with the policy of the planning authority to contain the geographical spread of the city. Such inconsistencies are seen as a major policy problem, and much policy work is concerned with the way different agencies handle the same policy issues.

To say that authority, expertise and order are the attributes of policy is not to imply that they are all equally present at all points in the process. In fact, they may operate against one another: for instance:

* The desire of the Minister for Education to exercise her right to make a decision about the school leaving examination (authority) may jeopardize the shared understandings so laboriously built up among schools, teachers, parents, universities, etc. (order).
* The criminologists know from careful research that taking a tough line on crime is not very effective (expertise), but find that the politicians think that the electorate favours this, and are more interested in the votes than the evidence (authority).
* Officials have negotiated a policy development which would be supported by all the relevant players (order), but the experts are insisting on a controlled trial before they give it their support (expertise).

So policy outcomes are likely to embody a continuing tension between these attributes.

Choice and structure

So far, we have spoken of policy in terms of articulate, conscious choice: policies are the choices which decision-makers have made, and they are clearly set out so that everyone knows them. Certainly, this is the way in which these authority figures would describe policy: it is their job to make policy decisions, and there are also jobs for others, advising them about the decisions they ought to make, and carrying out the policies once the decision has been made. But this may not give us an adequate analysis of the policy process.

In the first place, it sometimes seems difficult to divide the action into, on the one hand, clear policy decisions and, on the other, action taken to carry them out. As Schaffer and Corbett put it (1965: xiii), we do not find 'policy' as a thing apart, 'existing on a somewhat airless plateau' and quite distinct from 'a jumble of activities among the lower foothills'. Rather, it is a point of relative firmness built into a continuing flow: 'an obligation for some, a structural factor for other participants'.

What is described as policy may be clearly grounded in an authorized decision, but it may have its origin in practice: what can be done conveniently and systematically, what works, what is consistent with the expectations that others have of us. This pattern of behaviour may have the tacit approval of those in authority, but it is stretching the term to describe it as their 'decision'.

In any case, some would argue that having a formal policy decision is only the beginning of the policy process, and the critical thing is what happens as a consequence. It is easy to say, 'It is company policy to care for the environment', but does anything change as a result? What resources are allocated to environmental care? Are any staff allocated to the task? What happens when there is a clash between maintaining production and caring for the environment? For this reason, some would argue that policy has to be understood not in terms of intent, but of commitments.

> I shall use the term 'public policy' to refer to the substance of what government does; to the pattern of resources which they actually commit as a response to what they see as public problems or challenges warranting public action for their solution or attainment . . . I do not pretend that all students of public policy would agree with the meaning which I attach to this term, but then I do not consider that goals, intentions, principles, decisions, wishes, objectives or anything else that has been seen as constituting a public policy represents an appropriate usage of the term.
>
> (Dearlove 1973: 2)

In this perspective, policy must be understood not simply in terms of officially proclaimed goals, but in terms of the way activity is patterned among a wide range of participants, so that people know what is going to happen. Goal statements may be significant, but they are unlikely to tell the whole story, and their absence does not mean that there is no policy. The players in the game learn how things are done, they learn how the world is viewed, what is regarded as the problem, and what can be done about it. In this respect, occupations are an important source of pattern, and different occupations make sense of the action in different ways: a production engineer and a wildlife biologist will know quite different things about a proposal to extend a factory into a piece of adjoining bushland, and are likely to reach quite different conclusions about whether it is consistent with the statement, 'It is company policy to care for the environment'. In this perspective, the essential thing about policy is not the aspirations, but the effect they have on the action: policy is, in Schaffer's words, 'a structured commitment of important resources'.

Of course, making statements about policy goals is one of the important ways of committing resources, but it may not be sufficient, and it is certainly not the only way. The most important form of commitment is inertia: what we did last year is the best guide to what we will do this year. The budget tends to express this commitment, and carry it forward from year to year. The organization chart represents a particular commitment of resources: having a Department of Agriculture or a Consumer Affairs Bureau or an Office of Small Businesses reflects recognition of these interests, and offers a base for further claims. All of these would have to be counted as part of the structured commitment of important resources.

What we can see here is an ambiguity in the concept of policy: a tension between choice and structure. To describe policy as the choices of authorized decision-makers implies that the action follows from the decision: they could have chosen something else, and different action would have followed. But the experience of the policy process is often that it is the flow of action which throws up the opportunities for choice, and that the scope for choice is limited by the action already in place and the commitments which it embodies.

To take an example, in a country with an established system of technical schools, there will be decisions to be made about budgets and staff levels and new facilities, but it would be difficult to decide that vocational education should be conducted in the workplace rather than in schools. So much has already been committed to the system of technical schools – there are buildings and specialized staff and graduates who do not want the worth of their qualifications to be questioned – that it would be very difficult to close the schools down completely. It would not be impossible, but it would require enormous effort. Over time, policy innovations become institutionalized – in the form of bricks and mortar, the names of organizations, and job titles – and the commitment to maintaining them becomes very strong.

So the demands for decision-making emerge from the existing

system, and the scope for choice is limited by the commitments that have been built upon previous choices. And in this case, the initial choice might have been an agreement a century ago to pay a small stipend to a couple of part-time instructors at one school. And that decision may well have been generated by the flow of action: for instance, the employers might have been doing the training them-selves, but decided that they would like to pass this responsibility to some public authority, and the relevant decision-maker agreed to provide the relatively small sum involved, on the basis that this was consistent with other forms of public support for education. The large system of technical schools was built on this very small foundation. A choice was made then, but it was not a choice to have the outcome which we now see.

The point here is not that structure gets in the way of choice: the two dimensions of the policy process are inextricably linked to one another. Unless the policy decision could shape the action, there would be no point in making it. Unless the action could be linked to some policy statement, it would be difficult to secure support for it. But the two dimensions operate against one another: making choices challenges the existing structure, and having this structure limits the opportunity for choice. So there is a structural tension between the two in the policy process and, as a consequence, a lot of ambiguity.

Policy and labelling

It might seem that the ambiguity begins with the concept of policy itself: there has been much discussion in this chapter about how the term is used, but not what it actually means. This is because 'policy' is a term used by practitioners as well as academic observers. Imposing a definition which satisfies the observers but which failed to take account of the way practitioners use the term would be a self-defeating exercise. We must make our own judgements about how to use the term, but we need to take account of how it is used in practice.

We need to note first that 'policy' is a term which frames the action rather than simply describing it: it labels what we see so that we can make sense of it in a particular way. To say, 'Our policy on the young unemployed is in total disarray' is to highlight some things rather than others – e.g. young unemployed people as such, rather than the supply of jobs or the state of the economy – and to assume that the activities of different agencies (e.g. those responsible for education, social security, employment, policing, human rights, etc.) should be consistent with one another, and directed towards the solution of the identified problem (in this case, the position of young unemployed people).

At the same time, it directs attention away from other dimensions of the action. It directs attention to young unemployed rather than older unemployed, or young apprentices. It focuses attention on the implications for the young unemployed of the activities of schools or the police. But these agencies might see their primary task as being to run a system of universal education, or to keep the peace and apprehend lawbreakers, and view the situation of the young unemployed as a side issue. To talk about 'policy on the young unemployed' is to frame the action in such a way as to make it a central issue rather than a side issue.

To state that 'policy' is a particular way of framing the action implies that there are alternatives, and there certainly are. Perhaps the most obvious is 'politics', and 'management' or 'strategy' would be others. The distinction between these terms will be discussed in more detail later (Chapter 6), but we can note here that in ordinary usage, 'politics' seems to denote a continuing struggle for partisan advantage, whereas 'policy' implies a settled, considered choice. 'Management' (like 'strategy', 'corporate planning' and 'vision') is a term which originally was mostly applied to commercial organizations, but in recent years has become widely used in government and non-profit organizations. Many would claim that it is not really an alternative to policy, but is simply concerned with the ways in which policy objectives can be efficiently and effectively pursued. Others would argue that in practice, the stress on 'letting the managers manage' means an increase in the autonomy of managers, and a reduction in the scope for authority figures to determine policy.

But perhaps the main alternative to policy as a way of framing the world might not even be recognized as a label: we could call it 'practice'. People do things in ways that make sense to them, and there is no formal prescription about how they should act: they have operational autonomy. The existence of this sort of autonomy is sometimes overlaid and reinforced by claims about professional expertise: that it is inappropriate to have policies which override professional judgement. For instance, if a student threatens a teacher with a knife, should there be a policy that this student be suspended, or should this be left to the professional judgement of the school staff? Teachers may prefer to be able to use their own judgement, but officials of the education department would feel more secure if there was a standard practice which all teachers followed: a policy. (In one education department, it was estimated that there were over 500 such policies.)

Policy as a concept in use

This discussion has gone some way beyond the common-sense understanding of policy as a thing: a clearly stated (or at least generally understood) statement of intent on behalf of the organization: e.g. 'our policy on the level of immigration'.

Certainly, policy in this sense is (or can be) important, but we need to go beyond this. If statements like this are significant, it is because of the extent to which they shape practice. We need to ask what shapes practice, and how the idea of 'policy' plays a part in this.

We have seen in this chapter that the concept of policy mobilizes particular values. It expresses values of instrumental rationality and of legitimate authority. It presents action in terms of the collective pursuit of known goals, so that it becomes stable and predictable. And it sees these goals as being determined by some legitimate authority.

In doing this, the concept of policy both explains and validates the action: it explains what people are doing, and it makes it appropriate for them to do it. So it is not simply a descriptive term: it is a concept in use, and understanding 'policy' means understanding the way in which practitioners use it to shape the action.

But it is also a concept in use for observers: we use it as a way of interrogating organized activity – particularly, but not exclusively, in relation to public authority. It leads us to ask who is involved, in what settings, how action is framed, and what the significance is in this process of the idea of authorized purpose – that is, to ask questions about policy as a process, and not simply an outcome.

Further reading

There is an enormous amount written about policy, and one of the best guides to it is Wayne Parsons' systematic and encyclopaedic text, *Public Policy: an introduction to the theory and practice of policy analysis* (1995). This should be supplemented with a close reading of the daily newspaper, for evidence of the way in which policy is established, sustained and contested.

2

Who Makes Policy?

It is as though there were a political gateway through which all issues pass. Disputed from the moment they are in sight of it – and more hotly as they approach – they pass (if they pass) through, and drop out of controversy for a time. Managing the procession are certain 'gate-keepers' – not just the Cabinet of the day, but bureaucrats, journalists, association heads and independent specialists camped permanently around each source of problems.

(Davies 1964: 3)

One of the most seductive terms in the study of policy is 'the policy-makers'. It has a clear ring to it, and conveys an impression of a known group of evident and purposeful decision-makers determining the course of action.

But the concept often seems clearer than the practice to which it refers. The people who are identified as policy-makers often report that they do not seem to be out on their own, making something; rather, they find themselves presiding over an extended array of people with varying levels of interest in the question and quite distinct perspectives on it. They may find that their own ability to determine the outcome is quite limited, and they might want to include some of these other people as 'policy-makers'. In this case, it is more fruitful to suspend one's judgement about who (if anyone) is 'making policy', and concentrate on identifying the people who are participating in the policy process, how they got there, and what they do, and then determine whether we would want to identify any of them as 'policy-makers', and if so, on what basis.

How do participants get there?

To identify the participants, it is useful to go back to the elements of policy that were identified in the first chapter: *authority*, *expertise* and *order*. Because these are the elements of policy, they act as gatekeepers, each giving different people a basis for participation in the policy process.

Authority as a basis for participation

Authority is the best place to start, because the most obvious basis for a claim to a place in the policy process is the possession of legitimate authority. Policy is described as the work of 'the authorities'.

Just who is seen as the authority figure in policy-making depends on the detail of the particular case. Sometimes, it is a single individual: 'The Minister has decided . . .' or, 'The Secretary-General had determined . . .' But often, it is a collective body which is seen as having authority: the Cabinet, the Board of Directors, or the National Council.

In some cases, it may be the members of the legislature which are seen as holding the authority to make policy. Some writers, particularly in the US, are inclined to see a policy as being expressed in a piece of legislation; it follows that the legislators who voted for this legislation are 'the policy-makers'. In Westminster systems (such as Australia or the UK) where the executive can usually count on party discipline to keep the legislators in line, this use of the term is less common (but see Jackson 1995 on the decline of executive control of parliaments in Australia). But there is still widespread concern that the courts may make decisions on policy matters which should be for the legislature to determine. It is the legislature which has the authority to decide. The courts (it is argued) should not pre-empt the authority of the legislature.

In any case, when policy authority is seen as resting in some collective body at the top of the system, the question is how policy business gets to them. It may be that the Cabinet makes policy about education (for instance), but to paraphrase Marx, they do not make it as free agents, in times and circumstances of their own choosing. It would be extremely rare for the Cabinet to make a policy decision on education other than on the recommendation of the Minister for Education and, normally, the Cabinet's role in the

making of policy would be to accept the Minister's recommendation (or – less commonly – not to accept it, in which case the
Minister has to go away and try again). And the Minister's recommendation almost always originated with specialist officials further
down the line.

But to say that the Cabinet's role in policy-making is to accept or
reject the recommendations of specialists does not mean that it is
not 'really' making policy (with the implication that the 'real'
policy-makers are the people who draft the recommendations).
The policy process involves mobilizing the authority of the Cabinet
in support of the programmes of officials, and while it is possible to
divide the participants into 'real' policy-makers and subordinates
(or into 'real' policy-makers and well-publicized rubber stamps),
this may not sharpen the accuracy of our analysis.

The point here (and this keeps cropping up in the study of policy)
is that terms like 'policy-making' are not neutral, technical terms:
they are also part of the resources of the participants. The officials
want to get the Cabinet's endorsement of their plans in order to
strengthen their hand in dealings with other interests. For this
reason, they want to emphasize the Cabinet's role. It may be that
the proposal was approved by Cabinet on the basis of a one-minute
presentation by the Minister which no one was interested in discussing, but the outcome will be presented as, 'The Cabinet has
decided . . .'

Rather than dividing the policy world into 'policy-makers' (who
have authority and make decisions) and 'others' (who haven't and
don't), we should see 'authority' as a construct which frames the
world in particular ways, and gives particular sorts of standing to
people to participate in the policy process. It means that ministers
are there as of right, whereas the others have to establish their right
to be there, and to do this in ways which defer to the standing of
ministers. The specialists are there to advise their minister, and
experts from outside the bureaucracy have to find a minister to
whom they can direct their advice. The specialists' plans are
couched as submissions for the approval of the ministers, who are
seen as having a moral pre-eminence on the strength of their authority. 'In the end', it is said, 'the minister must have the last word.'

But then who has the first word? Putting it like this raises questions about what happened before the issue got to the attention of
authority figures like the minister. We would probably find that the

issue had been around for some time, and a number of people and organizations had been involved. The notion of authority gives these participants a particular standing in the game: the minister has the last word (which may mean that the minister doesn't come into the story until people are ready for the last word), the Education Department, as the main advisers to the minister, have a central role in managing the process, the Faculty of Education at the local university may be called in but has no right to be there, various sorts of organized interests may seek to have their say, and unorganized individuals (such as the parents at the local school) will probably have no place at all. This does not tell us how likely it is that particular people will participate, or how significant they will be (this will be discussed again under Expertise and Order), but it does help us to understand the relationship between the formal presentation of policy as authorized decision-making, and the experience of the participants.

We should also note that the flow may run both ways: top-down and bottom-up. Authority figures like ministers may be trying to pass directions down the line, but lower-level participants may be trying to pass business up the line, seeking authoritative endorsement for their plans. To do this, they have to relate to the structure of authority: schools wanting action on some policy issue would probably press their case through the Education Department, where they are 'insiders', but parents wanting action would be more likely to seek out the central parent organization as a body which has the authority to speak for parents. And an immigrant family with no social networks and limited English would probably find it very difficult to use either of these channels to make their voice heard on a policy matter.

Authority, then, frames the action, in ways that make it easier for some people, and more difficult for others, to take part in the process.

Expertise as a basis for participation

But policy is not only about authorized decision-making, it is also about problem-solving, and this constitutes another basis for participation: having expertise that is relevant to the problem.

The first question here is what sort of expertise – and what sort of experts – might be relevant. Expertise is not generic and free-floating, but has a specific focus: expertise about health, for instance, or welfare, or transport. This focus is sharpened by the nature of the institutional homes (as it were) for expertise: there is likely to be a government agency responsible for health, another for welfare, and another for transport. Responsibility for policy in any given area will be claimed by some functionally defined group of experts.

But there are likely to be a number of institutional homes, inside government and outside it, for any particular form of expertise, and the experts in government will probably have good links with those outside. The institutional specialization we have noticed in government is matched in the universities (which locate their expertise about these fields in different departments, often in different faculties) and in professional organizations. So the health experts in government are likely to have established links with health experts in universities and professional organizations, and also with voluntary bodies, companies and international organizations, and their links with their fellow health experts are likely to be stronger than their links with (say) the transport experts in government.

And the links run both ways. A company may respond to the emergence of environment protection policy by establishing its own environment protection branch, and would expect that its own experts would establish a good relationship with the environment experts in government, in order to get a better idea of the expectations of government, and in the hope that the company's own concerns will be taken into account in the policy process. When community groups demand a policy response on environmental problems, they look to the environment experts in government for a sympathetic hearing, and one of the first demands of such groups is that there should be (if there is not one already) an environment protection agency – an institutional location in government for their policy concern.

So expertise becomes an important way of organizing policy activity. People who are concerned with a particular policy area develop a special knowledge about it, and come to know who shares that knowledge: who the people are that they can talk to about it. There may well be newspapers or journals which they all read, or associations to which they tend to belong. They may have different ideas about what to do about the problem, but they recognize that they are all addressing the same problem. So analysts of the policy process see them as a significant grouping in the policy process: an 'issue network' or 'policy community'.

But we cannot assume that for any and every policy question there is a clear field of policy-relevant expertise. Different fields of expertise may have different ways of addressing the same question. Take drunkenness, for instance. Some experts would see this as a health problem, and would discuss what might be done to combat addiction and to help people to take better care of their health. Experts in welfare might be more concerned about the impact of the drinking on the life of the drinker and the welfare of those around him or her. They may be more concerned with measures to address the drain on the household budget, the threat of the drinker losing his/her job, and the likelihood of domestic violence. Other experts might see drunkenness as a problem of public order: people's drinking becomes a matter of policy concern only when it has an impact on other people's enjoyment of the public sphere, and the concern is with how to regulate public behaviour. And there would be some experts who would not see any policy problem: why should there be any policy response to the fact that people indulge (perhaps to excess) in drinking? Why not eating? Or gambling?

This shows not only that there can be different expert answers to the same policy problem, but also that it cannot be assumed that it is the same problem. These different bodies of expertise are not only generating responses to the problem: they are framing the problem in the first place. A body of expertise is a way of recognizing problems as well as a way of addressing them. And this is not a neutral process: it has implications for the allocation of resources. If drunkenness is seen as a problem of personal health and addiction, it would be appropriate to put resources into health care and education. If it is seen as a matter of public order, it might be appropriate to give additional powers to the police. So the way that the problem is framed is closely linked to who might have policy responsibility for it, and what resource claims might be made as a consequence.

In any case, the particular policy problem may overflow the categories of expertise which are being brought to bear. The care of old people, for instance, could involve a wide range of functional experts: in health, welfare, housing, transport – even taxation. Old people are more prone to illness, and often end up being kept in hospital because they could not cope by themselves at home. But with some help in the home, perhaps some renovations (e.g. replacing stairs with a ramp, installing handrails), they would be able to do so. The policy task may be how to mobilize the different sort of expertise that are scattered around the place, and not simply those which are 'indigenous', as it were, to the agency given responsibility for the area.

Moreover, it may not simply be that the policy problem involves a number of the existing pools of expertise: there are times when we can see new expertise being developed to challenge the existing pattern of policy knowledge. Environmental policy offers a good example. Some people were concerned about the impact of social and economic change on what might be called the amenity of ordinary life, and this came to be referred to as 'the quality of the environment'. This was a new term for something which had previously been without a label, but it took root, and became part of 'ordinary knowledge'. There also emerged specialized knowledge: academic research and professional expertise about 'the environment'. This found an institutional home in the universities and in environmental protection agencies. As it became established, it was used to challenge both the expertise and the practices of the existing players. For instance, it became common to require an Environmental Impact Statement of all new developments. This meant that engineers wanting to build a new road had to address themselves to a different question, and justify their plans in terms of a different body of expertise.

Order as a basis for participation

Policy is concerned with making organized activity stable and predictable. We may have a policy that children are not allowed to start school until they are five years old; this means that we avoid tension-filled encounters between school principals and anxious parents, and all the affected parties – children, parents, teachers, educational planners – know the situation. Within organizations, creating this sort of order is generally seen as a problem of control: how to ensure that the policy which has been created at the top is carried out through the organization, and how to avoid, on the one hand, bureaucratic rigidity and, on the other, excessive slack.

This perspective has been challenged by some writers who point out that for people lower down in the organization, the policy-making of the people at the top may not be sufficient to make their jobs stable and predictable, and that they may have to construct some order themselves. 'Street-level bureaucrats' in direct contact with the clientele of the organization – like judges in lower courts, schoolteachers and police – will work out with the clientele and other relevant participants (e.g. lawyers) how the service will operate. For this reason, some would argue that at their own level, these people are also making policy.

This need to create order is even more apparent when we look at the policy process across organizations. As we saw in the discussion of expertise, most policy questions extend across organizational boundaries. The care of the aged will necessarily involve a range of functionally defined organizations – e.g. those concerned with health, welfare, housing, transport, etc. If a policy on aged care is to generate predictability, it must involve these organizations.

Creating predictability becomes even more difficult when we take into account constitutional divisions. The national government may take responsibility for transport, but leave health with regional governments subject to national guidelines; housing may be the responsibility of a public corporation not under direct governmental control, and welfare activity may be carried out by regional and local governments and by non-governmental bodies. In this context, the question is not simply, 'Who needs to be included?', but also, 'Who must not be left out?' – i.e. whose exclusion would frustrate the policy or simply make it pointless?

Even when the constitutional responsibility is quite clear, the process of creating order may involve a number of hands. For instance, it might be agreed at the governmental level that 'each school is responsible for creating and implementing its own discipline policy', but making school discipline predictable would call for the involvement of a number of parties. Within the school, the list would include teachers, students, the school Principal, the parents, but it would also stretch outside the school to take in the expectations of the police, welfare authorities, the courts, and the practices of other schools. So constructing a school discipline policy would be very much concerned with the creation of order.

It is not simply that policy areas happen to cut across organizational boundaries: they may have been created with this intention. As we saw in the discussion on expertise, the whole idea of environment policy was a challenge to existing policy fields and the expertise on which they drew, compelling the various players to think about their activities in terms of an overarching set of values. Heritage policy, EEO policy or family policy would be other examples. They often originate outside the central policy framework – among community groups, professional associations, consultative bodies, etc. – and get support in part because they offer the prospect of a way of managing demands for an official response. If ministers find that they are always vulnerable to demands that they protect some historical building from development, they are likely to find considerable value in a heritage policy which to some extent defines and limits what can be expected of the government.

So it is not surprising that a great deal of policy activity is concerned with creating and maintaining order among the diversity of participants in the policy process. It seems to be not so much about deciding, but more about negotiating. And the negotiations focus less on alternatives between which we must choose, and more on common ground on which we can converge. The process is likely to be fine-grained and long-running. The participants work out a resolution of one set of problems, but new problems replace them, and they mobilize their collective problem-solving skills to address the new problems.

Making policy through collectivities

One consequence of this is the emergence of what might be called 'policy collectivities' – that is relatively stable aggregations of people from a range of organizations who find themselves thrown together on a continuing basis to address policy problems, who (in Davies' words) are 'camped permanently around each source of problems'. These may or may not be formally recognized, but they can play a very significant part in the policy process.

Often, the linkages among the participants are formally recognized. The interdependence of functionally organized officials – e.g. between health, welfare and housing – is fairly obvious and can result in several different sorts of official response. One is the creation of formal links between these agencies, such as inter-departmental committees. These bodies, either *ad hoc* or permanent, offer a way for these agencies to cooperate with one another. They also offer scope for them to resist one another: if the agencies see themselves as being in a competitive struggle with one another, the dynamics of inter-agency bodies is likely to be (as one study put it) 'politics between departments' (Painter and Carey 1979).

The other common official response is to establish a consultative body which will include not only the functional officials, but also participants from other governmental bodies and from outside government – e.g. from business, community organizations and the universities. These bodies give an opportunity for participants from a diversity of organizations to discover the extent to which they can support one another. They also help to constitute the thing for which they are called into being: the Barley Industry Advisory Council is a major force in getting farmers, traders, processors, association officials and bureaucrats to see themselves as part of something called 'the barley industry', and to think in terms of policy for the industry. These bodies are less likely than the inter-departmental committee (which finds it difficult to escape from the continuing internal struggle for resources) to produce a negative, defensive reaction.

Policy collectivities do not have to be formally recognized to be significant, and even where they are, not all of the relevant partici-pants may have been included on the formal body. But there may be a shared awareness among the participants of who the relevant people are in their line of business, even if there is no formal body to which they all belong. And outside observers may see the stability and pattern in the process even if the participants are not conscious of it. In fact, it has been observers of the policy process who have shown the most interest in identifying and labelling the policy collectivity, but unfortunately they tend to have used a variety of terms – e.g. sub-governments, policy communities, issue networks – and it has not always been clear whether the different terms denote different things, or are simply different labels for what are essentially the same phenomena. The terms that have been used tend to highlight different aspects of the process.

Some convey images of *power*. One of the earliest labels applied to a policy collectivity was the term 'iron triangle', which was a term from the Vietnam War applied as a metaphor for the way policy was made in regulated industries in the US. There (it was argued), policy was not made by the President or the regulatory body which he had appointed, but emerged in the interaction between the

regulatory agency, the industry association, and the relevant con-
gressional committee. The term conveyed both the strength of the
policy collectivity, and the relative weakness of the regulatory body
when acting on its own. This metaphor was extended by the term
'sub-government', which admitted a wider range of participants
into the policy collectivity, but again presented it in power terms: it
is the group that governs.

Others focus on *linkage* – and specifically, on the way that making
links forms networks. Some writers object to talking about the
policy collectivity as whole (e.g. to using the term 'community')
because, they say, it doesn't operate as a whole; when something
comes up, people make links with relevant others. The network
that is formed in this way, they argue, can't be thought of as an
organization: participants know the people near them in the
network, but don't act in terms of the network as a whole. And networks are very specific: the network which emerges over school
buses might be quite different to the one that forms over school
discipline, so rather than talking about a 'policy network' in relation
to schools, we might identify a number of 'issue networks'.

But the most common image of the policy collectivity has been
that of *community*. This suggests intimacy and trust: policy is made
among people who know and trust one another. This does not mean
that there cannot (as in any other community) be ignorance, mis-
understanding and conflict. But it is an image which stresses the
extent to which stable collective action is linked to mutual understanding: there needs to be some mutual understanding to have any
collective action, and the practice of working together reinforces
this understanding.

This image also draws our attention to the knowledge that policy
collectivities share. They are drawn together by their shared awareness of a particular policy area. In some cases, this may be a new
way of understanding the world, as happened with the emergence
of environmental policy. For this reason, researchers studying the
way policy was made in relation to global warming have talked
about the emergence of an 'epistemic community': i.e. a group of
people who understood what was meant by global warming and
why it was a problem. This does not mean that they would all agree
on what should be done about it, but they did not have to persuade
one another that something needed to be done.

It is useful for analytic purposes to distinguish between power,

linkage and community as elements of the policy collectivity, but
these are not mutually incompatible, and there is no reason why
more than one element should not be present in any particular case.
Coleman and Skogstad (1990) argue that a policy community has
two elements: a 'sub-government' and an 'attentive public' – or in
terms of this analysis, a power-focused centre, and an epistemic
community on the periphery. Sabatier and others argue on the basis
of a number of cases that a policy community contains two 'advocacy coalitions' in competition with one another – i.e. that there are
epistemic communities being mobilized in the contest for power
(Sabatier and Jenkins-Smith 1993).

It is important to remember that these terms are essentially
metaphors, introduced to help us make sense of the complexity of
the policy process. They focus our attention in particular ways. In
particular, they direct our attention to the social and interactive
dimensions of the policy process, as distinct from the linear and
hierarchical perspective which underlies much discussion about
policy-making. But they are constructs, not naturally occuring
phenomena, and should not be seen as definitive and mutually
exclusive categories.

Expanding our focus from, 'Who makes policy?' to, 'Who participates in the policy process?' gives us a more complete picture, but
it is important not to assume that it is a game in which anyone can
and does play. In the first place, not all those with an interest in a
policy question will necessarily have a place at the table, and even
if they do, not all seats are the same. Those concerned may have to
establish their right to participate, and some writers distinguish
between 'insiders' (who will be involved) and 'outsiders' (who
would like to be), or between (as we have noted) a 'sub-government' of insiders and an 'attentive public' outside.

In the second place, participation is not a neutral question; who
participates in a policy issue helps to shape what the issue is. As we
saw, different participants are likely to have different perspectives
on the question. Doctors are likely to see drunkenness as a question of personal health care, whereas the police are likely to see it
as a question of public order. To the extent that doctors have a
dominant voice in the discussion, the policy problem will be defined
in health terms; to the extent that drunkenness is seen as a health
issue, doctors and other health professionals will be seen as the
appropriate people to discuss it. In this sense, the problem and the

participants are 'mutually constitutive': the one reinforces the other. Neither who the 'decision-makers' are, nor what problem they are addressing, are self-evident phenomena: they are constituted in the policy process.

Further reading

A good account of the experience of a 'decision-maker' is Richard Crossman's *Diaries of a Cabinet Minister* (1975). The assumption that authority is the basis for participation in policy underlies much of the writing but is often unstated; Parker (1960) gives a clear summary of the argument. Much of the discussion of expertise as the basis for participation has related to the position of professionals in bureaucracies; see, e.g., Laffin 1986, also Benveniste 1973. A good account of the way that Environmental Impact Statements were used to contest the dominance of professionals can be found in Serge Taylor's *Making Bureaucracies Think* (1984). The discussion of order among policy participants has come to focus on the concept of the 'policy community' and the variants on it. The term 'iron triangle' comes from Ripley and Franklin (1984), and 'sub-government' from David Truman (1971); the distinction between a sub-government and an 'attentive public' was made by Coleman and Skogstad (1990). The idea of the policy collectivity as a network was introduced by Heclo (1978) and developed in America by Laumann and Knoke (1987) and others, and in the UK by Marsh and Rhodes (1992); there is a valuable critical review in Dowding 1995. The literature on the 'policy community' is extensive; Atkinson and Coleman (1992) give a useful review. Richardson and Jordan (1979) clearly set out and illustrate the argument. Analysts of international environmental policy-making extended this analysis to the idea of an 'epistemic community', which is discussed extensively in a special issue of *International Organization* **46**(1) (1992). The propensity of different sorts of experts to constitute policy problems in distinct ways is discussed in J.R. Gusfield's study of drink-driving, *The Culture of Public Problems* (1981).

3

Where Is It Made?

Finding policy: the map and the experience

We saw that it was easier to talk about 'the policy-makers' than to say exactly who they were, and we encounter the same difficulty in identifying where policy is made: in principle, it is quite clear, but in practice, the task becomes quite difficult.

The clear principle is that policy is made at the top, and passed down the line. There may be specialization of tasks among the policy-makers, so that one is responsible for education policy and one for health policy, and there may also be delegation downwards, so that subordinate officials can deal with less significant policy issues. But there is a single chain of authority, and a clear decision from which the action flows.

The experience of the policy process is more complex. It is often hard to find the top – or at least, the bit of the top that is relevant. If, for instance, the policy question is about the provision of bus services for school children, we could expect at least three elements of the government to show a close interest: the Education Department (whose students stand to benefit), the Transport Department (which might be expected to provide the buses) and the Finance Department (which will be concerned about the cost). But it would not necessarily be clear which of them (if any) was responsible for this matter. In addition, there would be a number of participants outside government wanting to take part in the discussions: the Parents' Association, the private bus companies, the non-government schools, the bus-drivers' union, and perhaps others.

Consequently, we might find that although in the end there was a 'government decision', it was preceded by intense negotiation among the interested parties to try to agree on an outcome which all of them would find acceptable. The question is then, 'Where did the decision get made?' In the Minister's office, when she signed the recommendation to Cabinet? In the meeting of interested parties, governmental and non-governmental, at which everyone agreed what would go into that recommendation? In the Cabinet room, where the recommendation was agreed to without discussion, along with 27 similar ministerial recommendations?

We could say, 'All of the above': policy is being shaped all along the line. On the other hand, one can argue that it does not become policy until it is endorsed by the Cabinet. This points to one of the difficulties with the concept of policy: the term can be used in a broad sense to refer to the process which gives shape to what the organization does, or in a narrow sense to refer only to particular authorized statements which express this direction. In formal terms, the policy is the statements, but to understand these, we need to know something about the process which gives rise to them and makes them meaningful. In the same way, a statement of the country's industrial relations policy will be found in the platform on which the winning party was elected and the subsequent official statements of the Minister, but these words have to be interpreted in the light of the way that government agencies, unions and similar bodies, lawyers, international organizations and others interact with one another to shape practice relating to employment – that is, the process which gives meaning to the official statements.

The constitutional map

There is no easy way out here: we have to recognize that 'policy' refers both to the authorized statements and to the process which produces them. This means that we will need to look in more than one direction to find it. When we think in terms of the authorized statements, we look to office-holders at the top of the organization, individual (the Minister, the CEO, the Executive Director) and collective (the Cabinet, the legislature, the Board of Directors). When we think in terms of the process, we ask, 'Who are the people who have an interest in this question, and to what extent are they able to take an active part in shaping the action? Are there organizations to represent them? Are they incorporated into the structure of decision-making? Are they involved in giving effect to the decisions?' What we are doing here is identifying the stakeholders, as they are sometimes called, but recognizing that this tells us what we are looking for rather than what we will find.

Policy and government

Since the range of potential participants in the policy process is so wide, it is convenient to start with the authorized decision-makers, and then look more widely. There are likely to be a number of official participants, as we have already seen. In business and non-government organizations, it becomes harder to know who might become involved, partly because the term 'policy' is less common. Non-government bodies tend to use different terms to refer to processes which in government would be called 'policy'. They might speak instead of 'mission statements', 'corporate goals', 'strategic planning', and 'positioning'. So it makes sense to start with the governmental participants, and then ask who else should be included in the action.

This is consistent with the mainstream literature in public policy, which identifies the source of policy as 'the government'. Policy is 'whatever governments choose to do or not to do' (Dye 1981: 1). This has a crisp ring to it though, as we shall see, it raises questions about how policy questions arise in government. It sees policy as the work of government, which seems to be common sense, but there are times when the government appears to be quite remote from the process. For instance, in many countries, the dairy industry is subject to extensive control, but these controls are determined and enforced by bodies set up by governments but not controlled by them, composed largely of representatives of farmers and others in the industry (see Farago 1985; Grant 1985; van Waarden 1985). In many fields of activity, similar bodies are constituted so that the industry (or the profession, or the charitable group) can run their affairs without involving the government, which wishes to keep itself at arm's length from the body concerned (Streeck and Schmitter 1985). It seems misleading to describe what emerges from such bodies as 'government decisions'.

The executive as the site of policy-making

Even if we put this point to one side for the moment, and accept for the sake of the argument that policy-making is the work of the government, this still leaves a very wide terrain to survey. Political scientists distinguish three separate branches in government: the executive, the legislature and the judiciary. In which one is policy made? Certainly, the executive is the most visible, containing the most senior of the people who make policy statements – including the Prime Minister, the President, and the members of the Cabinet – and it would appear to be the obvious location for policy-making. Executive work seems to be dominated by the taking of policy decisions: in Westminster systems, there is an elaborate procedure which involves framing policy proposals which filter up the bureaucratic hierarchy, receive the approval of the minister, are discussed with other departments, and finally go before the Cabinet. Once they are approved there, all the ministers are committed to supporting them and they become 'government policy'.

On the other hand, it may be misleading to see these public and prestigious figures as the people driving the policy process. They tend to serve in a range of positions, for relatively short periods – perhaps two to three years – in fields of which they may have little prior knowledge. They preside over a large body of officials who are likely to have more knowledge and experience of the policy area than the person at the top, and there has been an enormous amount of discussion in the literature about the relationship between political leaders and officials. The political leaders will probably have ideas of their own about the direction in which they want policy to go, but the officials will have more ideas, more specific ideas, and more sense of which ideas will work. So more often than not, the driving force for policy will be the officials behind the political leader. So as a location for policy-making, 'the executive' would include both the political leaders and the officials in the agencies which operate under the leaders' authority.

The legislature as the site of policy

But some would see 'policy' as signifying more than the decisions of political leaders and officials. They would argue that policy is expressed in laws – even that a law *is* a policy – and that, therefore, the place where it is made is in the legislature. This view is most common in America, where the sharp constitutional distinction between the executive and the legislature encourages the view that the legislators are making the broad policy choices, which the executive then puts into practice, and that it is therefore the legislators who are the policy-makers.

In parliamentary systems, where party discipline normally ensures that the legislation which is passed is that of which the executive approves, it is less plausible to present the legislators as 'the policy-makers'. But at the same time, there is a good deal of 'policy activity' in and around the legislature. Debates in the legislative chamber offer an opportunity for the critique and justification of policy. The public hearings held by committees of the legislature provide an opportunity for exploring policy alternatives with stakeholders. If we see policy in the broader sense, as process, then clearly the legislature is one of the places where it can be found.

The judiciary and policy

The third branch of government is the judiciary, and while judges would usually deny being policy-makers, there are clearly times when significant policy activity is taking place in the courts. In many countries, particularly (but not only) in federal systems, contested policy issues are likely to find their way into the courts. The decision of the US Supreme Court in the cases of *Brown* v. *Board of Education* (on the equal rights of black Americans) and *Roe* v. *Wade* (on abortion), and the Australian High Court's Mabo decision (on indigenous land rights), were fundamental policy shifts which took place because participants took the issue into the courts and received a positive response, so we cannot exclude the courts from our definition of the location of policy-making. But the courts do not have as much legitimacy in the process as the legislators or the elected leaders, and generally claim that they are not seeking to make policy, only to interpret the law that is there.

In addition to the courts, there are now a number of other opportunities for pursuing policy questions through judicial channels as new specialist tribunals are established, particularly in such fields as immigration, consumer rights, and trade practices. It can be said that they are simply concerned with implementing policy but, to a large extent, the policy is what they implement. To have a policy that restraints on free trade should not be allowed unless the tribunal finds them to be in the public interest means that the tribunal's interpretation of what is in the public interest becomes the substance of the policy. So judicial forums – both courts and tribunals – are another location for policy activity.

Broader organizational maps

The implications of organizational fragmentation

Government is divided into functionally specialized agencies – a department of immigration, a department of education, a taxation department, etc. – but it is harder to divide the work of policy-making into such neatly segmented boxes. Addressing a policy question like alcohol and driving, for instance, calls for joint activity involving different hierarchies – e.g. the police, the roads department, the health department, etc. In terms of the model, we might expect that the officials concerned would go to the source of the authority – the Cabinet – and secure endorsement for their activity, which would then impose an agreed outcome on all ministers and their officials. But research suggests that officials are relatively reluctant to go to Cabinet to settle a dispute between departments until they have exhausted the possibility of negotiating their own agreement with other officials (Painter 1981). They do not want to make everything depend on clear lines of authority. So 'making policy' includes negotiation with officials in other functional areas.

Negotiation is also needed with other levels of government. Authority in government is not neatly concentrated at one point, but is in many respects diffused through the system. There is usually some dispersal of authority to local and regional levels of government, though the extent of dispersal varies: in federal systems, it is most pronounced and best protected, but even in unitary systems, there is rarely a complete concentration of authority at the centre. And increasingly, policy activity is being carried out in international arenas, such as the European Union, UN agencies and the World Trade Organization.

Although we may speak of the 'machinery of government', not all government organizations can be seen simply as the tools of the authorized leaders. The police, for instance, often have considerable autonomy of governmental direction. Some bodies need a degree of autonomy of central authority simply to operate. The courts, for example, need to be independent of the government if they are to be seen as neutral arenas for dispute settlement. While universities may be publicly funded, they are loath to see themselves as the instruments of the governments which provide the funds. And though governments have often run trading enterprises such as railways or telecommunications services, these bodies are given considerable operational autonomy, to minimize the possibility that their commercial viability will be compromised by political pressures.

Policy work also often involves mobilizing authority from outside government. Generating policy on marijuana use and driving, for instance, may well involve representatives of the medical profession, the churches and civil liberties advocacy groups, each of which can claim to speak with authority on the medical or moral implications of policy proposals. In the same way, it may involve authority from outside the country concerned. International agreements, for instance, may be mobilized to lend authority to proposed domestic policy moves; for instance, there may be an international agreement about drugs which has something to say about marijuana use which can be adopted in putting together a policy on such questions as marijuana and driving.

Making common ground for the policy participants

Because the policy process is so dispersed, the participants take steps to draw it together. We saw in Chapter 2 that we could identify 'policy communities', made up of those making a claim to be involved in policy in particular areas, and who had learned how to work together. These originate as informal relationships and may stay that way, but there is a tendency for the participants to try to institutionalize them – that is, to give them some organizational form.

A first step is often to identify a single voice to speak for the clients or beneficiaries of the policy – for instance, the formation of a single farmers' association to speak for farmers. This is likely to be encouraged by government because it is easier for government to deal with organized interests than unorganized ones, and it is worth providing a subsidy to (for instance) a national consumer organization so that there can be a single voice to speak for this very diffuse interest.

Beyond this, there is a variety of institutional envelopes for policy communities: advisory councils, industry conferences, policy forums, etc. These are ways of formally recognizing the policy significance of the wide range of people who become involved, and integrating them into the official structure. These bodies vary in the extent to which they have their own, autonomous organizational existence. They may simply be called together from time to time by the minister, but they may be more securely institutionalized: they may have their own offices and staff, and may even be recognized in the legislation. The organizational arrangements for the recognition of policy communities vary widely, and there is no particular logic to them; what is constant is that the participants in the policy process tend to develop stable relationships across organizational boundaries, and try to provide some recognition and stability of these relationships in the official structure, so that they can continue to be used in the crafting of policy.

Policy: where do we look for it?

It might seem that this discussion has been interesting but inconclusive: it's still not clear where policy is made. It seems to be like the 'floating crap game' in the Damon Runyon story: everyone knows it's going on, but no one actually sees it happening. So where is policy made? The answer is, 'It depends' – but we can be more specific and less frustrating than that.

It depends on what we mean by policy

We have seen that 'policy' conveys a number of meanings – notably authority, expertise and order – and that the term can refer to quite different things, ranging from a specific announcement by a minister (a 'policy decision') to the broad pattern of collective action in some field (e.g. 'social policy'). To the extent that policy is seen as conscious choices by authorized decision-makers, then we would look for it in the formal institutions of government: in the decisions of Cabinet and of the ministers, formally recorded and officially proclaimed: 'This is the government's policy on greenhouse gases.' To the extent that policy is seen more broadly –

like 'social policy' – we would want to look more broadly: not simply at what the government says, but at how its resources are deployed, at the values that the participants hold, and at what other organizations outside government are doing. For instance, Castles has noted (1991) that in Europe, people who are too sick to go to work are generally covered by benefits in the state welfare system, whereas in Australia, the employer is obliged by law to continue paying the sick worker, up to a certain length of time each year ('sick leave'). To give a good account of social security policy, we would need to ensure that it covered both sorts of provision. This means that we would need to look more broadly at the practices of other participants as well as at the statements of authorized leaders.

It depends on the nature of the issue

Where we look for policy depends on to what extent issues can be handled 'in-house' – i.e. by officials of the lead agency – and to what extent 'outsiders' have to be involved. This is a matter of degree rather than a categoric distinction: most policy issues would call for some degree of 'outside' input, whether of other officials or of non-officials. But it is useful to think of three distinct levels of 'permeability'.

We could call the first level 'the inside job': here, policy matters are the concern of the agency with responsibility for the area, and there are no other significant participants with an interest in taking part in the policy process or the capacity to do so. Where 'policy' is taken to mean 'Standard Operating Procedure' (e.g. 'our policy is not to act on complaints unless they are submitted in writing'), we can see that this might not be of much interest outside the agency. But to the extent that few outside the agency are interested in the policy question, then the place to look for policy is the agency – not only what it says, but what it does, how it is organized, and the matters to which it pays attention – and to some extent, the political leaders who preside over it.

The second level can be termed 'the specialist community': the policy area is of concern outside the agency, but mostly to specialists, and it does not attract a great deal of public attention. This facilitates the development of links among these specialists; these may be more or less stable, and to the extent that they are, analysts may refer to the pattern of linkage as a 'policy community', 'issue network', 'sub-government', etc.

The third level could be called the 'open contest', by which we mean that the issue is one which is of interest to more than specialists, and is likely to be the subject of public debate, with the present state of play, the various alternatives, and the positions and dispositions of the participants being discussed in the media, perhaps in the legislature. In these circumstances, the policy process is more likely to lead to formal institutional action – e.g. a ministerial statement, or the introduction of new legislation – which is relatively open to view, though the negotiation which preceded it is less visible.

To talk about these as 'levels' is to make a somewhat artificial distinction, but one which helps us to focus our attention on the different sorts of arena in which the action takes place. However, we have to remember that there are no fixed barriers between the levels. In the example cited of the agency requiring complaints to be in writing, we can see that if someone complained to the Ombudsman about the implications of this rule, even the internal procedures of the agency might become matters of outside, perhaps public, concern. Participants in the specialist community can always 'go public' if the proceedings in the specialist arena are not satisfactory. Conversely, political leaders in the public arena are likely to seek to consign a difficult policy question to 'the experts' (i.e. the specialist community) and ask them to work out a solution.

It depends on the dimension of the policy process

Up to this point, we have accepted a quite wide range of usages of the term 'policy', from the narrow (e.g. 'health policy' as meaning 'what the present minister has stated as policy') to the broad ('health policy' as 'the whole set of arrangements, understandings and commitments governing the provision of health care'), without asking much about the relationship between them. Why is there so much variance in the terminology, and why has this variance been tolerated in this discussion, rather than clarified at the beginning? The reason is that there are two dimensions to policy, the 'vertical' and the 'horizontal', and the different usages belong to different dimensions.

The vertical dimension sees 'policy' in terms of the transmission

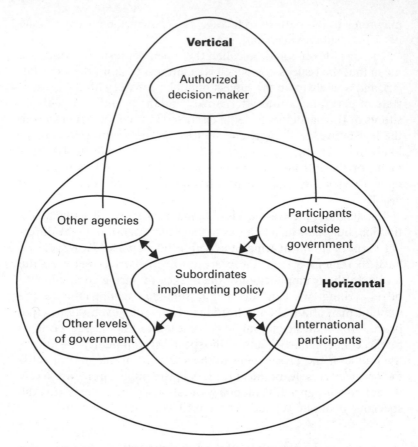

Figure 3.1   The vertical and horizontal dimensions of policy.

downwards of authorized decisions. The authorized decision-makers select courses of action which will maximize the values they hold, and transmit these to subordinate officials to implement. (It may be that the subordinate officials sent the courses of action up for endorsement, but the decision-makers still had to give their authority.) It is a dimension which stresses instrumental action, rational choice, and the force of legitimate authority. It is concerned about the ability or capacity of subordinate officials to give effect to these decisions (the 'implementation problem') and with ways of structuring the process of government so as to achieve this compliance.

The horizontal dimension is concerned with relationships among policy participants in different organizations – that is, outside the line of hierarchical authority. It recognizes that policy work takes place across organizational boundaries as well as within them, and consists in the structure of understandings and commitments among participants in different organizations as well as the hierarchical transmission of authorized decisions within any one organization. It is concerned with the nature of these linkages across organizations, with how they are formed and sustained, with the interpretive frameworks with which the participants understand policy questions, and the institutional formations within which these are mobilized.

The two dimensions are not alternatives: rather, each tends to assume the other. The implementation of the authorized decision calls for the cooperation of relevant others outside the line of hierarchic authority. And shared understandings reached on the horizontal plane must be given effect via the instruments of the vertical dimension: the ministerial decision, the policy directive, the regulation. But the two dimensions offer different answers to our question, 'Where is policy made?' In the vertical dimension, policy is made when the authorized decision-maker gives assent, so attention is focused on the ministerial office, the Cabinet room, the Parliament. In the horizontal dimension, policy emerges from a complex set of relationships among participants, marked as much by continuity and ambiguity as by clear choices, so it is hard to identify a point at which policy is 'made': rather, we see a continuous process of framing and re-framing.

> The public policy process is then a multi-person drama going on in several arenas, some of them likely to be complex large-scale organisational situations. Decisions are the outcome of the drama, not a voluntary willed, individual, interstitial action. Drama is continuous. Decisions are convenient labels given *post hoc* to the mythical precedents of the apparent outcomes of uncertain conflicts.
>
> (Schaffer 1977: 148)

Both dimensions are part of the policy process, so we cannot discard either, which means that we have to accept that there is more than one answer to our question.

The other lesson to be drawn is that since the source of policy is clearly wider than 'the government', the discussion about the

relative role of government, business and non-government organizations becomes clearer. Policy is clearly 'public', but this is not the
same as 'governmental'. Policy involves the exercise of governmental authority, but government officials and authority figures are
not the only people involved, nor are they necessarily the leading
players. Making policy on the steps to be taken to anticipate and to
cope with flooding in a river valley is likely to involve not only the
agency concerned with emergencies, but also a number of other
government departments, the defence forces, regional and local
authorities, business associations and a range of community groups.
The authority of government is being mobilized, but so too is the
authority of these other bodies: the policy process is concerned with
the structuring of commitment both inside government and outside
it.

In this context, the reluctance of commercial and non-governmental bodies to use the term 'policy' becomes less puzzling: they
are less concerned with the structuring of activity on a broad scale,
and more concerned with their own activities, for which they can
find other words. They are less likely to describe their Standard
Operating Procedures as 'policy', as a government agency would be
prone to do. When they get drawn into the broader web of public
policy – e.g. in terms of the environment or EEO – they are more
likely to use the term 'policy' – e.g. 'our policy on environmental
protection' – than they would be in areas that are more clearly
'internal' (e.g. market coverage).

This means that 'policy' remains something of a moving target,
but we do have a clearer idea of why this is so, and just what it is
that we are looking for: the structuring of action on a broad frame.
The results of this activity may be proclaimed by authorized leaders
in the government, using formulae like, 'It has been decided . . .',
but while it is important that these figures 'enact' the policy moves
in this way, they are not the only, or even the most important,
figures in the action. So while our enquiries might start there, we
can expect to look further to get a full understanding of the process
of steering which is captured by the word 'policy'.

Further reading

What to read next depends on which way you look. Most policy
texts have a section on the 'institutions of government', framed in

the vertical perspective: Considine (1994) and Howlett and Ramesh (1995) are good examples. These fairly traditional accounts of the policy world arc now being shouldered aside by the large body of writing on horizontal linkages among policy participants – i.e. of 'networks' and 'communities'. Rhodes (1992) and Coleman and Skogstad (1990) are good examples of the 'policy community' approach, and Sabatier and Jenkins-Smith (1993) a good critique. There is a tendency for this writing to focus narrowly on the characteristics of particular patterns of linkage rather than to analyse the horizontal dimension as such (see, e.g., van Waarden and Schmitter 1992), and the student of policy might learn more by reading some of the organizational literature on the horizontal dimension of organization (e.g. Perrow 1986; Scott and Meyer 1991) and applying it to the policy field.

4

What Is It For?

The question, 'What is policy for?' is not often asked, perhaps because the answer seems obvious. This is all the more reason that it should be asked, because it brings out the taken-for-granted in the analysis, the elements which are not subject to close scrutiny because it is assumed that everyone shares them. It also brings out what some would call 'the relevant counterfactual' – i.e. what are the alternatives to policy? What would we have if we didn't have policy?

The dominant paradigm

The dominant paradigm in the study of policy sees it as the exercise of authority to achieve collective purposes. Policy is to be understood in terms of the pursuit of goals: our policy is what we want to achieve. Certainly, the assumption that policy is a purposive course of action (Anderson *et al.* 1984: 4) underlies the mainstream definitions of policy. Lasswell and Kaplan define policy as 'a projected program of goals, values and practices' (1970: 71), and Friedrich puts it bluntly: 'It is essential for the policy concept that there be a goal, objective or purpose' (1963: 70).

To see policy as the pursuit of authorized purposes appeals to 'common sense' because it fuses two widely-held assumptions: first, that government is there to pursue goals, and secondly, that these goals are the optimal improvement in the welfare of individuals.

Perhaps the second assumption – that the goals of government should be to maximize the welfare of individuals – should logically come first. Here, the dominant paradigm in the policy literature is in the tradition of Jeremy Bentham and the Utilitarians, who held that the justification for government lay in its capacity to advance the greatest happiness of the greatest number. This approach, extended by the concept of Pareto optimality (the best action is that which makes someone better off and no one worse off), has been at the base of mainstream policy analysis (see Jenkins-Smith 1990: ch. 1). Much attention has been devoted to finding ways to calculate the 'best' policy option, generally based on a calculation of the relative advantage to different interests of the achievement of the desired goal of each of the options.

Discussing what goals the government should have does of course assume that government is the sort of creature which can have and pursue goals – that is, that it is a single entity, with a mind of its own: coherent, instrumental and hierarchical. The organization can be treated as a whole: it exists to carry out purposes, and these are defined at the top. In this perspective, policy is the specification of these purposes, and it is implemented when the purposes are achieved. In this perspective, we could see the policy process as consisting of a number of stages:

1 Determining goals. The first question is what the goals are. In this perspective, goals are determined by the decisions of authorized leaders. If they wish to act rationally, they need to be clear about the objectives they wish to achieve.
2 Choosing courses of action. Having clarified the goals, the leaders select the courses of action which will realize these goals, bearing in mind the relative costs of carrying out each course of action.
3 Implementing these courses of action. Other workers then have to implement the courses of action that have been chosen, and the rest of the organizational process is described as the implementation of these choices.
4 Evaluating the results. The outcome of the implementation of the decision can (and should) now be evaluated: 'Was the decision thoroughly and economically put into effect?' (efficiency evaluation), and, 'Did the implementation of the decision have the expected impact on the problem to which the policy decision was addressed?' (effectiveness evaluation).
5 Modifying the policy. If necessary, the policy is then amended in the light of the evaluation.

Purpose as a guide to the policy process

This 'linear' presentation of policy as an orderly progression from
objective to outcome seems so logical and unexceptionable –
common-sense, almost – that it might seem surprising that practitioners should report that it is at variance with their experience.
They find the policy process to be more complex and ambiguous.
Here, one of the puzzles facing both analysts of policy and practitioners in policy fields is the disjunction between the way people
talk about policy and the ways they experience it. People talk about
policy in terms of the pursuit of a clear set of agreed goals: 'The
objectives of this policy are . . .', but they often report that in their
experience of the policy process, it is difficult to see these agreed
goals: agreement is hard to achieve or to sustain, objectives are
unclear, and the process is about continuing negotiation and a
search for commitment as much as it is about the achievement of
known goals.

Participants find, for instance, that even within a single organization, it is not always evident what the goals are that are being
pursued. This may be because there are no clearly articulated goals,
or if there are, they do not appear to be terribly significant in determining what people do. There may be a statement of corporate purposes in a glossy book, but most people in the organization either
haven't seen it or don't see it as having much to do with the way
they do their jobs. Or there may be several statements of policy
purpose which may be inconsistent with one another, e.g., 'The
goals of our immigration policy are to protect our cultural integrity,
to promote family links, to facilitate the migration of labour, to
protect the employment of the existing workforce, and to meet our
international obligations.' These are all valid statements of the
desired outcome, but it is likely that pursuing one would be at the
expense of another, so it is not very illuminating to describe the
action as the pursuit of these policy objectives.

In fact, the presentation of organized activity as the pursuit of
defined purposes has a slightly unreal character to it. It is not that
statements of purpose cannot be found, or do not command assent:
it is that there seem to be a number of other processes at work.
People in organizations want to show their professional skills,
execute the Standard Operating Procedures of the organization,
and maintain stable relations with the organization's clientele. In

doing this, they may well refer back to statements of purpose, which clearly have some significance, but it would be misleading to see their activities simply as attempts to achieve these purposes.

Nor can it be assumed that the activity will be evaluated in terms of defined objectives. There may be a formal evaluation in terms of goals, but activity is also evaluated in the ordinary working of the organization. It is possible that the work of a schoolteacher might be evaluated in terms of the accomplishment by the pupils of the defined learning objectives, but is likely that there will also be a more mundane way of evaluating it: 'Are there any disciplinary problems?' 'Is the level of classroom noise within normal expectations?' 'Are there any complaints from parents?' 'Do the pupils progress to the next grade without difficulty?', etc.

This 'process-oriented' way of evaluating the activity of the organization may run alongside more formal 'objective-oriented' exercises in evaluation. Education inspectors, school principals and parents are likely to have different ways of evaluating what goes on in the classroom. By extension, we could say that they have different educational objectives, but this would require us to translate their perspectives on process into clear objectives, and this may not be very helpful. It would not surprise us to find that the school Principal prefers classrooms to be quiet, disciplinary problems to be few and parents to be uncomplaining, but does this mean that these are his or her objectives for the school?

But in any case (as this example suggests), the question of purpose usually cannot be limited to a single organization. As we saw in the last chapter, the policy process includes many participants, and they are likely to have distinct, possibly contradictory, views on what the programme should be like. It is not simply that they have different ideas on what to do about the problem: they may have quite distinct views on what the problem is. As we saw from the example of public drunkenness in Chapter 2, different functional specialists will interpret it in terms of their own expertise and activities, and generate different ideas of what would be an appropriate policy response. Determining policy goals is therefore not a matter of a context-free group of 'policy-makers' determining what the goal will be for all the participants: there is a range of interested parties who will have their own analysis of the problem, and will be seeking wider support for what they see as the most appropriate course of action.

This means that the link between the action and the policy goals becomes problematic: we cannot assume it. There may be a number of policy goals in circulation. Even when the activity is being undertaken in response to some articulated policy objective, it may be at variance with another objective. Action taken in pursuance of the policy objectives of opening up labour markets and meeting our international obligations may act against the objectives of protecting employment and maintaining our cultural heritage. And articulated policy objectives may cut across the other cues for action. The articulated objective of having important but controversial topics like sexuality and HIV–Aids discussed in the schools may be at odds with the Principal's desire to avoid antagonizing significant numbers of parents. So rather than interpreting all the action as the implementation of some policy objective, we need to ask what the link is between objective and action.

Alternatives to purpose

That purpose is only one of the possible ways of understanding the policy process can be seen if we consider some of the alternatives.

For instance, while policy can be said to be about purpose, it is also about *routine*: 'The department's policy on late essays is . . .' means, 'This is the routine which we have adopted for dealing with this situation.' This is easy to parody as the emergence of bureaucratic procedures which have no relation to (in this case, educational) goals, but all organization is about routinization – developing known and predictable ways of dealing with events. Organizations develop Standard Operating Procedures, and these are likely to be different in different organizations. Allison points out that the differences between the Standard Operating Procedures of the Pentagon, the CIA and the State Department are critical to an understanding of the American policy process during the Cuban missile crisis (Allison 1971). They had different ways of acquiring, processing and evaluating information, and came up with quite distinct understandings about what was happening and about what response was appropriate. Policy practitioners may well recognize two different types of policy: explicit rationales and purposes as one type, and the recognized regularities in the organizational process – the Standard Operating Procedures – as the other.

Looking at it in another way, we can see that policy is also about *structure*. Organized activity is shaped not only by the purposes which it seeks to achieve, but also the nature of the organizational forms through which it happens. For instance, a policy of a high school Parents' and Citizens' Association to orient students to the workplace is likely to look rather different to the same policy pursued by the head office of the Education Department. The local P and C is likely to operate in a more individual, perhaps idiosyncratic, way, tapping known individuals and working through personal contacts, whereas the Education Department, which has to deal with a range of schools and knows little about their links with the workplace, is likely to operate more formally, to define standard procedures, and to seek out central organizations of employers with whom to negotiate. In this context, the key questions are not, 'What do we want to achieve?', but, 'What work do we do?', 'Who does it?', and, 'What commitments of resources underlie these arrangements?' These are the questions that are familiar to policy practitioners: not just, 'Is this an authorized objective?' but, 'Whose responsibility is this?' and, 'What resources – staff, money, the attention of those higher up – can they call on to do it?'

As we noted, some writers see policy entirely in these terms – e.g. as 'a structured commitment of important resources' (Schaffer 1977). In this context, we can understand why reformers seek changes not only to the formally-stated goals of the organization, but also to the structure. Environmentalists, for instance, may demand that the road-building agency not only adopt a policy goal of protecting wildlife habitats, but also that it set up a Habitat Protection Unit in the agency, staffed by biologists, to keep attention focused on this policy objective. Similarly, as we have seen, they may call for their concern to be built into the routines of the organization – as with the requirement for all large construction projects to be accompanied by an Environmental Impact Statement which makes specific reference to habitat.

Another perspective on policy sees it not in terms of the selection of goals to be achieved in the future, but as the *interpretation* of our present situation and action. Rather than the question being, 'Where do we want to go?', it is, 'Where are we now, and what do we do about it?' March and Olsen (1989: 23) compare two alternative ways of understanding action:

Anticipatory action	*Obligatory action*
1 What are my alternatives?	1 What kind of a situation is this?
2 What are my values?	2 Who am I?
3 What are the consequences of my alternatives for my values?	3 How appropriate are different actions for me in this situation?
4 Choose the alternative that has the best consequences.	4 Do what is most appropriate.

This perspective ties in with what has been said about routine and structure: these both have an important part to play in our making sense of the world.

> The accountant asks: What does an accountant do in a situation such as this? The bureau chief asks: What does a bureau chief do in a situation such as this? Institutions are constructed around clusters of appropriate activities, around procedures for assuring their maintenance in the face of threats from turnover and from self-interest, and around procedures for modifying them.
>
> (March and Olsen 1989: 24)

In this perspective, then, policy is concerned with making sense of action, which helps us to deal with the fact that the action may have come first, and the definition of an objective may have followed. It was not, for instance, that an immigration policy was made, and immigration followed, but rather that the fact of immigration impelled people to create policy on this subject. This may have involved drawing together action in a number of different fields – labour markets, education, social security, citizenship – into a perspective called 'immigration'. In this perspective, policy is about the way that the action was framed under a particular label.

Purpose as a heuristic tool

But while this purpose-oriented model of policy may not be a perfectly accurate representation *of* the policy process, it appears to be significant *in* the process. The participants in the policy process mobilize this model to make sense of the action in which they are engaged. It frames the action in a particular way which makes it both comprehensible and legitimate. It offers a framework which enables people and values to be appropriately located and recognized.

We can see, for instance, that this purpose-oriented model makes sense of the policy process as the application of *authority*. It begins with the determination of authorized goals, and explains the rest of the organizational process as the pursuit of these goals, culminating with an assessment of whether those goals have been achieved. It explains the participants' place in the action in terms of their relation to authority: people can act together because authorized leaders have determined the collective purpose, which all the participants then work to achieve. These authority figures are then described as the 'decision-makers', the people who choose the purpose and the means to achieve it. Other policy workers are described by reference to, and as subordinate to, the decision-makers: they are offering 'policy advice' or providing 'decision-support'. And beyond them are the 'implementers', whose role is seen as carrying out the decisions of the authorities, possibly subject to the scrutiny of 'evaluators', who will report back to the decision-makers on whether their purposes have been achieved.

Because this approach gives such a central place in policy to the purposes of the authorities, it focuses attention on the way in which these purposes are selected, and gives rise to a 'methodology of choosing': analytical frames and techniques to guide the authorities towards the optimal choice. This includes not only specific appreciative routines like cost–benefit analysis, but also the ideas in which these techniques are grounded: the perception of policy in instrumental terms (i.e. what is done can be understood as a particular distribution of benefit), and the aspiration to find the right allocation of benefit through tests like 'Pareto optimality'.

This development of 'technologies of choice' directs our attention to the way that the purpose-oriented approach frames the policy process in terms of *expertise*: if policy is concerned with the attainment of goals, the central questions are what the goals should be, and in what ways they should be pursued. These are questions where specialist knowledge comes into its own. Should we have an industry policy? What are our goals in relation to urban growth? What is the best way to achieve our health care goals? Fields of specialized knowledge emerge which address these questions. 'Industry policy', 'urban policy', 'health policy' all become identifiable areas of expertise, with professional associations and journals and graduate courses, and those who possess this expertise can claim a particular standing in the policy process.

This immediately raises the question of the relationship between 'authority' and 'expertise' in the policy process. Who leads: the authorities or the experts? How can you make policy on health if you have not been trained in that field? Or do those in authority simply give voice to the views of the experts? The relationship is inherently ambiguous and potentially conflict-ridden, and in the folk wisdom of the policy world are proverbs which reflect (and serve to dissipate) this tension – e.g. the liberal sentiment that 'experts should be on tap but not on top', or the Chinese Communist assertion of the importance of being 'both Red [i.e. imbued with political authority] and expert'.

Moreover, as we have already seen, it is unlikely that there is a single, clear field of expertise in relation to any policy problem. It is likely that there are different sorts of expertise which can be mobilized, and that these will define the question in different ways. In the case of forest policy, for instance, it is likely that economists, foresters and ecologists may all have different answers to the question, 'What are our goals?', so that it is not simply a matter of the experts versus the authorities.

But this example points us to our third framework: the orientation to purpose can be mobilized to create *order* in policy fields. It is not (as we have seen from the forests example) that there *is* a clear and shared purpose underlying policy, but that participants accept it as proper that there *should* be. This means that they may confront the fact of the existence of different perspectives on the nature of the activity and what it is that is valued by asking, 'What are our objectives?'

Putting it in these terms invites participants to express their different perspectives in a comparable way. Such an invitation may produce a quite diverse set of goals, for example:

- 'to maximize the contribution of forestry to the economy'
- 'to derive the optimal sustainable yield from the forests'
- 'to maintain the forests as a habitat for flora and fauna'

– but expressing the different perspectives in terms of a goal makes it easier to deal with the fact of their diversity. The worth of each perspective has been recognized, and attention is directed to how to frame action in a way which recognizes the different perspectives. This is often done by trying to draft a set of goals to which all the participants can give assent, for example:

- 'to derive the optimal return from the community's forest resources while maintaining the natural ecosystems'.

Such statements tend to be very broad, and are sometimes dismissed as almost meaningless – 'motherhood statements' – because while all the participants may assent to them, they do not give us a clear guide to what will be done. But their meaning lies in the fact that they do exist, and that participants from all of the diverse policy perspectives can draw on them (in different ways) for support. In this way, the purposive framework is mobilized in the constitution of order in the policy process.

Purpose and management

Whether or not policy is built upon shared purposes, this notion plays a significant part in the management of organizations. Organizations tend towards differentiation – i.e. they are broken up into different elements, such as branches with different functions, and often geographical subdivisions as well – and managers are concerned with organizational cohesion: pulling these elements together. The discourse of purpose – policy goals, mission statements, strategic visions, corporate plans, etc. – can play an important part in this process. It spans the differentiation within the organization, and it creates a platform on which the different players can meet.

It can also help the centre to exercise control over the operative parts of the organization. It provides a basis for the centre to challenge the inertia of the operational elements of the organization. Functional specialists want to carry out their specialization: hospital doctors want to treat patients, water supply engineers want to build dams, town planners want to define standards, etc. Seeing policy as purpose enables the centre to contest the tendency of the specialists to want more of the same. It can ask, 'Is this activity the best way to get to some defined end?' Should we treat more patients in hospital, or should we be redirecting some of them into more appropriate forms of care? Should we cope with the increasing demand for water by increasing the supply, or could the policy objective of having an adequate water supply be satisfied by reducing demand – e.g. by increasing the price? Statements of policy purpose can be used as a point of leverage, an external reference point which the centre can use to manage the demands of the operational elements. They can be used as a way of rationing resources: how would this resource demand contribute to some stated set of policy purposes? In this way, the articulation of purpose becomes part of the process of control.

This link between purpose and control in organizations flows both ways. It is not simply that leaders in organizations seek control in order to accomplish purposes: people also articulate purposes as a demonstration of their claims of leadership. Would-be political leaders, in particular, are asked, 'What is your policy on x, y or z?', but in a range of organizational contexts, leadership is demonstrated by articulating purposes. This is part of the 'cultural construction' of leadership in organizations – i.e. it is what people expect leaders to do.

We can see, too, that the orientation to purpose can be important in negotiating relationships outside the organization. For instance, the justice agency might adopt a juvenile crime prevention policy, aiming to reduce the incidence of crime among young people, and seeking the cooperation not only of the courts, police, welfare agencies, but also of non-government organizations and the school system.These other bodies might have little interest in the incidence of juvenile crime – e.g. the schools are likely to see their role as being to educate children, and not to be a general agency of social control – but articulating a purpose to which few could object becomes a way of trying to mobilize support from a wide range of sources. Just as purpose can work to create common ground within the organization, it can operate in the same way across organizations.

Purpose and the policy process

This discussion has argued that while the idea of policy as purpose is important in the analysis of policy, the policy purposes which we encounter are not independent of the policy process and prior to it, but rather have to be understood as part of the process. Policy does not start with a purpose and proceed to action: people seek to make sense of the action, and frame and refine statements of purpose. It is a continuing process of interaction between the interpretation and the action to which it relates. Policy, we have seen, is a way of making sense of the action, drawing disparate forms of activity into a common framework. Our question is how this is done, and with what consequences for action, and more particularly, what is the significance of purpose in the action and in the analysis?

The assumption that policy is concerned with the definition and accomplishment of purposes is so grounded in the dominant paradigm of human action as instrumental rationality that it is not subject to the examination which it merits. It is taken for granted that social action is directed to goals, that policy is the pursuit of collective goals, and that policy statements indicate what these goals are. But observation of the policy process casts doubt on this assumption. Often, statements are so broadly-phrased, and contain such internal tensions and contradictions, that it is hard to see that action could be directed to their achievement. And observation of the organizational process does not suggest that it is best understood as the pursuit of clearly understood goals.

> Information is gathered, policy alternatives are defined, and cost–benefit analyses are pursued, but they seem more intended to reassure observers of the appropriateness of actions being taken than to influence the actions. Potential participants seem to care as much for the right to participate as for the fact of participation; participants recall features of the process more easily and vividly than they do its outcomes; heated argument leads to decision without concern about its implementation; information relevant to a decision is requested but not considered; authority is demanded but not exercized.
>
> (March and Olsen 1989: 48)

This suggests that while statements of purpose are highly significant in the policy process, we cannot see the action simply as the pursuit of these purposes. Explanations of policy as the careful progress towards a known goal validate action better than they explain it (March and Olsen 1989: 25). But purposive presentations of policy are important to the participants. Drawing as they do on the dominant paradigm of instrumental rationality, such presentations facilitate the mobilization of support for policy.

This reminds us that policy is about process as well as outcome, and about commitment as well as goals. Participants in the policy process try to build support for their activity, and statements of purpose facilitate this. But the broader and less specific they are, the more likely it is that they will attract support, so statements of purpose tend not to be very precise, and it becomes difficult to interpret the process as a quest to attain them. There are exceptions to this pattern – e.g. the Republican congressmen elected in 1994 described their (relatively specific) policy platform as 'a contract with America' – but statements of purpose in policy have to be understood in terms of their place in the present, as much as in terms of a future state to which the policy will lead.

Further reading

Since rational instrumentalism – the perception that policy consists of the pursuit of known goals – is deeply-rooted in the 'common-sense' understanding of the world, it tends to be assumed, rather than analysed, in the policy literature. Jenkins-Smith (1990) has a good discussion of this 'utilitarian assumption', and with Paul Sabatier (1993) argues that the dynamic of policy is coherence around values rather than the pursuit of agreed goals. March and Olsen (1989: ch. 3) is a useful critique of the instrumental assumption, and Kingdon's discussion of agenda setting (1984), and Edelman's analysis of the symbolic aspects of the political process (1988) are also valuable correctives.

5

What Happens to Policy?

Policy as the pursuit of goals

In the 'common-sense' view, policy has to do with choosing and implementing goals. We saw in the last chapter that while this was not an adequate description *of* the policy process, it was clearly significant *in* this process. It enables people to frame the action in particular ways: first, the making of a decision, then its implementation – and ideally, evaluation to ascertain that the intentions of the decision-makers have been accomplished. This is often represented as an endless loop:

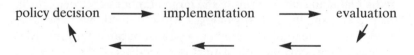

policy decision   ⟶   implementation   ⟶   evaluation

In this perspective, policy is seen as a cycle, with implementation and evaluation forming part of the policy process. We will start by discussing them in this perspective, but move on to look at them in a wider frame, as we did in the last chapter.

Implementation as a problem

In this perspective, policy is about choosing our goals, but it is also about choosing the means of accomplishing these goals: if we do *a*, then *b* will result. The policy embodies a theory of cause and effect. When the policy-makers' intentions have been carried out, the desired objective should have been achieved: this is

'implementation'. But if what we find on the ground is significantly different from these goals, then the policy has not been
implemented. This was the perspective taken in the pioneering
book on this subject, Pressman and Wildavsky's *Implementation*
(1973) whose subtitle gave it all away:

> *Implementation:*
> *How Great Expectations in Washington*
> *are Dashed in Oakland; or,*
> *Why It's Amazing that Federal Programs Work at All,*
> *This Being a Saga of the Economic Development Administration*
> *as told by two Sympathetic Observers*
> *who Seek to Build Morals on a Foundation of Ruined Hopes*

They asked why it was that the goals articulated by the policy-
makers in Washington bore little relation to what could be seen on
the ground in Oakland, California. When the question was put like
this, it was immediately and widely recognized to be a general problem: in all policy fields, there was a 'problem of implementation', in
that the outcome was likely to be quite different to the originally
stated intentions. So it was not simply a matter of determining the
policy goals: they had to be put into effect.

Pressman and Wildavsky explained the lack of implementation
in the Oakland case in terms of the large number of participants in
the process, and the diversity of goals. Most of the things to be done
needed to be 'cleared' at a number of points, because they involved
a range of participants with distinct perspectives of their own and
different levels of commitment to the policy objectives. The more
the policy depended on such 'clearances', the more likely it was that
the original objectives would not be accomplished.

This was also reported in other studies of implementation, which
also found a number of other causes for policies not being implemented: the original decision was ambiguous; the policy directive
conflicted with other policies; it was not seen as high priority; there
were insufficient resources to carry it out; it provoked conflict with
other significant players; the target group proved hard to reach; the
things that were done did not have the expected impact; attention
shifted to other problems, etc. Indeed, the literature is a little
depressing, because it is predominantly about 'implementation
failure'.

Response I: Complying with the model

There are several ways in which people have responded to this diagnosis of implementation failure: the first is about *compliance*: it looks for ways to make the experience of policy implementation more like the common-sense expectation. Sabatier and Mazmanian (1979) confronted the problem by reversing the question; instead of asking, 'Why is policy not implemented?' they asked, 'What are the conditions under which policy *will* be implemented?', and argued that these were:

- a sound theory of means and ends: if it is not true that doing *a* will bring about *b*, then the policy objective *b* will not be achieved
- unambiguous policy directives: if the policy is unclear, or there are multiple policy goals, then implementation becomes problematic
- leaders who are skilled and committed to policy goals: policy will not implement itself, but needs the efforts of leaders
- the support of organized groups and key legislators: opposition from such groups can easily block the implementation of policy measures
- no change in priorities over time: otherwise support for the policy may wane before it can be implemented.

This diagnosis of implementation as a problem points to a prescription for reform: have clear goals, and give someone the necessary authority to achieve them. Specifically:

- be clear about objectives, and about the contribution of policy to achieving them; make authoritative declarations of policy which are backed by thorough research and evaluation
- be specific: establish clear indicators of performance, and call for evidence of progress towards their accomplishment
- develop an orientation to outcomes, and reward people on the basis of the achievement of these outcomes; where possible, have quasi-contractual relationships with the implementers, such as the 'purchaser–provider split'
- structure the organizational arrangements to maximize the commitment to the policy of all relevant actors; try to vest responsibility for the implementation of policy in a single body – for instance, dealing with the policy problem of river pollution (which involves a number of functional and territorial bodies)

may require the creation of new authorities based on river catch-ments; and secure the commitment of those outside the structure of government whose cooperation is necessary
- review policy commitments regularly and make clear what the priorities are.

The implication is that more effort needs to go into making policy work: more research into the problem, more attention to 'policy design', and careful evaluation of the outcome.

Response II: Contesting the model

But it is also argued, both by observers and by practitioners, that the model is not a good guide to the policy process, and there is little point in trying to make the process like the model (see, e.g., Palumbo and Calista 1990). There may not be a clear link between means and ends: policy has to deal with 'wicked problems' (like homelessness, for instance) which have to be addressed even though it is not clear what would 'solve' the problem. People may support policies for different reasons, and so policy statements will tend to be non-specific, even ambiguous. Leaders will tend to give attention to the most pressing problems, and are likely to pay less attention to the implementation of a policy than to its formulation. The political system gives some participants incentives to oppose policies and creates institutional bases for them to do so. All these factors are variables, but it would be most unusual for policy par-ticipants to encounter the circumstances defined by Sabatier and Mazmanian as the conditions for successful implementation.

Some writers claim that the model is in any case skewed, a 'top-down' perspective on policy, which reflects the particular interests and understanding of managers and gives an inadequate picture of the policy process as a whole. Barrett and Fudge (1981), for instance, argue that while it is possible in conceptual terms to draw a clear distinction between policy and its implementation, in prac-tice there is a constant interaction between the managers at the top and the operatives at the workplace, and that it is quite inaccurate to see the relationship between the two as 'making' and 'imple-menting' finished policy. Rather, they say, we have to recognize that those who are giving effect to policy are also shaping what it is. So we should think in terms of 'action' and 'response', recognizing that

it is a continuing process, and that the initiative does not necessarily come from the top: a 'bottom-up' perspective shows that operatives are also making policy as they turn problems into routines,
articulate rationales for them, and seek the commitment of organizational resources.

It was also argued that it is unrealistic to see the implementation
of policy as involving only superiors and subordinates in the one
hierarchical organization. It is likely to require the cooperation of
other people, who may be in other governmental organizations
(which means that they are in other hierarchies), in organizations
but outside government, or who may not be organized at all. Both
formulating policy and putting it into practice are likely to involve
a range of participants, with their own distinct understanding of
what the policy issue is and what they hope to achieve. The
'bottom-up' critics pointed out that for the practitioner, an important part of policy work consisted of drawing these various participants into a common framework. In this perspective, while it is
appealing in some ways to see the policy process as the pursuit of
clear objectives, this may be an over-simplification, and from the
point of view of those involved, quite unhelpful.

For this reason, some analysts argue that the focus should not be
on the policy-makers and their objectives, but on the whole pattern
of relationships through which policy is implemented. Hjern and his
colleagues call this the 'implementation structure'. They point out
that in much of the literature on implementation, it is assumed that
all the elements necessary for success are contained in the organization that is responsible for the policy, and that if there are any 'relevant others' outside their organization, they should be brought
inside it: they refer to this as the 'Lonely Organization Syndrome'
(Hjern and Porter 1981). Implementation is only a matter of what
that organization decides to do. Of course, this is much easier, both
for practitioners and for observers: the focus is on the organization's policy, and other people are noticed in relation to that policy
– do they help or hinder?

But in this perspective, we lose sight of why the others do what
they do – helping or hindering the policy with which we are concerned may not be uppermost in their mind – and how policy participants do manage to work together even though they may have
different perspectives on the objective. Hjern and Porter suggest
that the focus should be not on a single organization, but on the

pool of organizations that are relevant for a given policy area. Any given policy question will involve people from a range of organizations – and not whole organizations, but a few individuals in each one. What draws them together is a programme of action to which all of them can contribute, and which makes sense to all of them, though not necessarily for the same reasons: they can agree on what to do without having to agree on why they are doing it. Hjern and Porter refer to these people as an 'implementation structure' – the grouping of participants who share a commitment to a particular programme. They make up a loose organizational form – some are more cohesive than others – with the members having enough discretion to make commitments about their own organizations' contribution to the programme.

Response III: Relating the model to the practice

The literature on implementation has tended to consist of two schools of thought talking past one another, with well-developed critiques of the other approach. The first writers, like Pressman and Wildavsky, took a 'top-down' position almost unconsciously: it was taken for granted that authorized policy should be put into place, and to the extent that 'outsiders' were noticed, they were obstacles to implementation. This provoked the objection from the 'bottom-up' school that the top-down presentation of the world was unrealistic and quite unhelpful in the real world because it ignored the extent to which policy developed out of this constant interaction, largely between 'top' and 'bottom', but also between 'insiders' and 'relevant others' – i.e. on the horizontal dimension – and that it was simplistic to think in terms of policy followed by implementation.

Some 'top-down' analysts responded that the 'bottom-up' analysis simply defined the problem of implementation out of existence. If there is no distinction to be drawn between policy and implementation, and everything is negotiated within the implementation structure, then 'implementation becomes a tautology: implementation was a success because what was implemented became the policy' (Linder and Peters 1987: 466).

But both the 'top-down' and the 'bottom-up' approaches are telling us something about implementation, and the problem is how to link them together. Wildavsky moved in the direction of the 'bottom-up' approach without actually abandoning his original position. His classic text *Implementation* (originally written with Jeffrey Pressman) went through three editions. In the first edition (1973), the underlying question was why the policy had not been carried out. The second edition (1979) retained most of the original text but added a chapter on 'Implementation as evolution', and the third (1983) had chapters on 'Implementation as mutual adaptation' and 'Implementation as exploration'. Sabatier (1986) conceded some of the points of his critics, and suggested that perhaps it was a matter of strategic choice: in some circumstances, the top-down approach could be taken, in others, it was more appropriate to use the 'bottom-up' approach.

The trouble is that there appear to be 'top-down' and 'bottom-up' elements in the policy process as such: there *is* a mobilization of authority, and there *is* a process of negotiation between those responsible for the policy and 'relevant others' outside. The question is how these elements are combined in our analysis of the situation. In other words, we are concerned with how the situation is *framed*: how do people make sense of it? (See Schön and Rein 1994.) Here, there are three important things to remember about policy:

• there is both a horizontal and a vertical dimension
• there is both an empirical and a normative component, and
• the language is part of the action.

The vertical and the horizontal dimension

As we have already noted, there are two dimensions to the policy process: the vertical and the horizontal. The *vertical* dimension is concerned with authority and hierarchy. Policy is seen as being about the choice and pursuit of objectives. Organization is seen as coherent, instrumental and hierarchical: it exists in order to carry out goals which are determined at the top – e.g., 'The department is only here to serve the Minister.' In this perspective, the key policy task is to determine objectives through analysis of the problem, and to assess (in advance or in retrospect) the effectiveness of alternative policy choices. Attention is focused on the efficiency with which these authoritative choices are transmitted down the hierarchy: how effectively is the policy being 'implemented'?

The *horizontal* dimension is concerned with the way that the policy process flows outside any given organization and involves people from other organizations, and with the implications this has for the nature of both policy and the process. It emerges from the experience of the participants that while the vertical presentation policy is clearly important, they find that much of the time they are concerned not so much with transmitting instructions within an organizational hierarchy, but with negotiating with people outside it who share an interest in the policy question, but have a distinct perspective on it and whose cooperation cannot be taken for granted. In this context, there is a good deal of ambiguity about objectives – can they be identified, how consistent are they with one another, and to what extent do they help us to make sense of the action? Policy workers are involved in developing and maintaining networks through which the various participants can relate their shared concerns to one another.

In the horizontal dimension, policy is a collective process: not the straightforward execution of a single idea, but continuing inter-action between a number of participants. The policy problem does not emerge automatically: it is recognized as the various partici-pants bring their different perspectives to bear. They will have dis-tinct understandings of the action, and a policy objective like 'sustainable development' may mean quite different things to en-vironmental groups and logging companies. 'Policy implemen-tation' is a label for the process through which these differing understandings encounter one another.

The point here is that there are different dimensions of the policy process, but that they may pull in different directions. It is not that one is 'theory' and the other is 'practice': both are essential ele-ments of the same process. The vertical dimension gives legitimacy: for example, officials in the environment protection agency can seek more staff in order to implement the goals announced by the government and enforce the statutes passed by the legislature. And the horizontal dimension gives efficacy: the officials know that in order to secure the change in practice which the official goal envis-ages, they will need to get the cooperation of industry organiz-ations, regional government bodies, the standards authority, environmental groups, their own inspectors in the field, and others. But it may be that producing a quick response for the minister (ver-tical) will alienate industry bodies whose cooperation is sought (horizontal), which will mean that the officials concerned will experience a continuing structural tension in their policy work.

Empirical and normative frameworks

The distinction between empirical ('is') and normative ('ought') statements is well-established in the social sciences, and is particularly significant in this context. The vertical dimension of policy is heavily normative in tone: it is located in a presentation of government as a hierarchy of authority, with its lower- and middle-level workings being traced back to potent symbols of legitimacy at the top: elected ministers, party platforms, statutes enacted by the legislature, etc. Officials and their offices are described as the agents of legitimate authority: enforcing legislation, executing Cabinet decisions, and advising ministers. It is important that the process be expressed in these terms – e.g., 'The Minister has decided . . .' – even when the decision was the result of an agreement between officials and representatives of the affected interests, and the Minister showed no interest and signed the final document without reading beyond the first page. Empirically, it may be that it is a decision of those affected, to which the Minister has assented, but normatively, it is the Minister's decision.

The participants recognize the existence of the two frameworks: the officials and the representatives know that the agreement they reach must also gain the assent of the minister, and the minister (usually) appreciates that it is unwise to exercise ministerial authority without prior consultation with those over whom it is being exercised.

The outcome is that there are different accounts of the same process in circulation. One account can be called *sacred*: it draws on the normative framework, and talks of the rational pursuit of legitimately chosen objectives: 'The policy objective is . . .' The other account is *profane*: it draws on the empirical framework, and talks about contest between agencies, about process and ambiguity (see Colebatch and Degeling 1986). Participants recognize that which account is used depends on the circumstances: when making a speech to Parliament, the Minister would be likely to use the normative account ('The government has decided . . .'), but this would be out of place in a planning meeting of officials. Journalists make stories out of the contrast between the normative and the empirical account ('What *really* happened').

The language is part of the action

This illustrates the way in which the language is itself part of the action. 'Everyone knows' that the experience of policy can be presented in different ways, 'sacred' and 'profane', and that it makes a difference which presentation is used. The 'common-sense', instrumental model of policy is part of the sacred: it is an essential element of the policy process, even though one would not want to use it as an empirical description.

What it does is to provide a framework for negotiation. It may be that empirically, policy in the area of (say) vocational training for the industrial workforce reflects the activities of industry and the training bodies more than any plans of the government as such, but since policy is expressed in terms of 'the government's objectives', this compels the interested parties collectively to seek the support of government, and to negotiate an outcome that can be presented in these terms. The shift from, 'The relevant interests have reached agreement' to, 'The government has decided' is important because of the signal it gives to the participants inside and outside government, and the resources (financial and other) which it commits.

In the same way, talk of 'the government's overall objectives' might seem empirically unrealistic, given that the members of the government spend most of their energy pursuing their individual agendas, and generally come together only to struggle over scarce resources. But having the concept of overall objectives enables them to conduct this struggle indirectly, as a struggle over symbolic statements about objectives – e.g. whether the objectives talk about 'growth' or 'equity' or 'sustainability' or 'competitiveness'. The words are broad, but the differences between them are significant, and the participants are trying to mobilize language in a way that supports their own perspective.

Implementation and framing

So the way in which the implementation problem is perceived, and what one might do about it, depends on the perspective being applied. In the vertical perspective, implementation means that authorized decisions at the top coincide exactly with outcomes at the bottom: it is a question of securing compliance. This is the (usually tacit) assumption on which much of the writing on the question is based: that the policy process is best understood as the formulation of goals by 'policy-makers', the selection of instruments to achieve them, and the assessment of the outcomes. This reflects constitutional models of government, and instrumental models of organization: it is seen as self-evident that 'those elected by the public to government should be able to place their policies into action' (Linder and Peters 1987: 465).

In the horizontal dimension, implementation is an exercise in collective negotiation: the focus shifts from the desired outcome to the process and the people through which it would be accomplished. In the vertical dimension, the focus is on the policy goals, and people and organizations come into the picture to the extent that they contribute to (or obstruct) these goals. The horizontal dimension recognizes that policy is an ongoing process, and that the participants have their own agendas and therefore their own distinct perspective on any policy issue. For instance, an employment agency may propose a system of traineeships as a means of getting the young unemployed back into the workforce. The Finance Department, which is concerned with controlling spending, may see it as a fresh and potentially expanding spending commitment. The trade unions (whose cooperation is important) may see it as a threat to traditional apprenticeships. And the young unemployed may see it as an allowance for which they may or may not qualify. All of these are realities which are relevant in the pursuit of this policy, and the implementation of policy will involve negotiation between these different realities as the various participants become involved.

This poses a difficulty for implementation: what is it that is being implemented? In the vertical perspective, there is a tendency to see 'policy' emerging pristine and fully formed from the head of a detached 'policy-maker', but in the horizontal, it is something which emerges in the course of interaction among the relevant participants. It is not that the policy was complete when it first emerged and was then at risk in the interaction that followed, but rather that it was this collective process which produced the policy. This changes the question about implementation from the execution of a clear objective, to the achievement of collective action which is compatible with the perspectives of all the relevant participants. This shifts the focus from the policy-maker – whether this is seen as an individual or an organization – to the process of interaction. It also recognizes the time dimension – i.e. that the process does not begin with a detached 'policy-maker' articulating a new policy and inscribing it on a blank sheet, but that it is part of a continuing game in which a regular cast of participants recognize and respond to policy questions. The game is not fixed – new players seek to be recognized, and there is contest over how policy questions are to be understood – but there is continuity as well as change, and policy initiatives have to take their place in this ongoing process, leading Sabatier to suggest (1986) that the time frame for the implementation of a new policy should be ten or twenty years.

In this context, the concept of implementation is a way of framing the action in a particular way. It highlights some things rather than others, and defines people and processes in relation to the policy under consideration. For instance, it defines the Regional Superintendent of Education as the implementer of the policy on multicultural education. The Superintendent may have had nothing to do with it and may see it as being of marginal importance, but by definition, he or she is the implementer of the policy. The teachers' union may be interested because of its concern that teachers being asked to do extra duties should get extra money – and it may see success as blocking the introduction of any new policy that is not accompanied by extra allowances. The parents' organization may see the new policy as an irrelevance and potential source of overload, and will be concerned to limit its impact on the core curriculum. The implementation of the policy also involves them, though they would not see themselves as 'implementers'. Implementation is not simply about achieving shared goals, but also about defining the meaning of the policy and the criteria of success.

Policy workers have to operate with all these ambiguities: they have to cope with the horizontal as well as the vertical, the normative as well as the empirical, and they are very conscious of the way in which terms are used to shape practice. They know that the vertical or the horizontal are not alternative ways of doing policy, but distinct and complementary perspectives on what is involved. The vertical dimension is a normative presentation of the process: it explains outcomes in terms of giving effect to the choices of authorized decision-makers. This is the proper outcome: that the directives of authorized leaders should be given effect. This is implementation. The horizontal dimension is an empirical presentation: it explains outcomes in terms of what can be observed. But it is not incompatible with the vertical: it is asking different questions. The participants know that the public presentation of any policy must be cast in the vertical: this practice is authorized. But they also know that authorization is rarely enough, and that authorized statements will usually follow a process of negotiation aimed at incorporating the 'significant others' into the final outcome.

Evaluation in the policy process

In the 'common-sense' model of policy with which the chapter started, evaluation completes the cycle: it enables policy-makers to know to what extent they are achieving their objectives, and to act accordingly. The common sense of evaluation is clear: if policy is concerned with achieving goals, then it is only sensible to check whether or not these have been attained. Managers want to be able to show that their programmes are effective.

It has become increasingly common for evaluation to be built into the policy process, particularly as part of the relationship between institutions: legislators may demand that the activities of officials are evaluated, control agencies (like finance departments) may demand evaluation of operating agencies (like departments of agriculture or education), and central governments may attach evaluation requirements to grants to regional or local governments or non-government bodies. And who can object to a systematic check on whether policy objectives are being attained?

This demand has fuelled the development of an elaborate methodology of evaluation, incorporating (as the Sabatier and Mazmanian requirements would demand) the policy objectives, the hypotheses about change, and ways of measuring outcomes. For instance, if the policy problem is seen as the high number of road deaths (road toll) among young drivers, a policy of incorporating driver training in the school curriculum might be instituted (i.e. the source of the problem is seen as low skill levels, which can be addressed by the training programme). The evaluation might measure the road toll among trained drivers after the programme was instituted, monitor a comparable group of untrained drivers, and compare the road toll among trained and untrained drivers, using measures of statistical significance. From this, the evaluators could form conclusions about impact of training on road toll, and the policy-makers could act on the basis of these conclusions – i.e. if it were found that the road toll among trained drivers was no different than among untrained drivers, then the training programme would be cancelled.

While evaluation may work this way, we may well find that there is a demand to maintain driving training in schools (or introduce it where it does not exist) despite the evidence that it does not appear to make any significant difference to the road toll among the young people who have been trained. It may be that the training is supported by school principals because it is a good way of keeping Year 10 occupied while their exams are being marked, by parents because they are always happy for the schools to do systematically things which they would otherwise have to do themselves, and by motoring interests because it smooths the way for young people to become car owners. In these circumstances, one could imagine that any attempt to close down the programme would be met with strong opposition, and outraged cries about the road death toll among young people, and the importance of driver education.

This example of evaluation in the policy process brings out some of the points that we have noted in the discussion of implementation.

Evaluation reflects the perception of policy
The form evaluation takes reflects the way the policy process is understood: is it a united pursuit of shared goals, or is it an attempt to achieve collective action among people who do not necessarily agree on goals? To the extent that the policy process is seen as goal-oriented, it makes sense to measure progress toward these goals systematically, and ideally, to measure relative progress under alternative routes. What works? What will get us there fastest? Most cheaply?

But if there is divergence over goals, agreement has to be forged at a more superficial level: we can agree more readily on what to do than on why to do it. What the driver training example suggests is not that people are pursuing shared goals, but that there is a variety of values (not necessarily shared, but not inherently inconsistent with one another) that can be mobilized to support a particular programme. This means that evaluation has to be concerned not simply with whether the policy is achieving its objectives, but also with what the policy means to people, and what criteria might be applied to it.

But even though people might have a range of reasons for supporting a policy, not all reasons are equal, particularly in public. 'Improves the driving skills of young people and saves lives' is a better objective – in that it commands wider support than 'gets the kids out of our hair while we mark the exams' or 'prepares the next generation of car buyers'. Here again, we find 'sacred' and 'profane' presentations of the same policy episode. Framing the policy in terms of its impact on the road accident toll is a meaning which is shared by all advocates, and which supports claims on resources.

The analysis is part of the action

This discussion of the driver training example shows that evaluation will always be a part of the action. It is mobilized in the policy process by some of the participants in order to affect the way resources are committed – perhaps by education authorities who can think of other ways to spend the money – and the way other participants respond in defence. This raises questions about the relationship between the analysis and the participants: should it seek to be *detached*, or should it be *engaged* in the process being evaluated? And if it is engaged, whose interests should it serve? The development of evaluation methodology has been largely in the tradition of positivist social science, with the evaluator like a fly on the wall, observing the action without being part of it. Care is taken to keep the collection and assessment of data separate from people conducting the activity being evaluated.

Critics argue that these scientific aspirations are unreal, since detachment is not feasible, and that in any case it is not desirable. They point out that evaluation is primarily a form of control, exercised by managers over subordinates, and that this power relationship cannot be ignored. Moreover, if the point of the evaluation is to change the way some people do their work, rather than excluding them from the evaluation process in the name of scientific objectivity, they should be drawn in so that they identify with it and are committed to it, rather than ignoring or resisting it as a piece of outside interference.

The conflict between detachment and engagement pervades the literature on evaluation. It is reflected in the distinction between 'summative' evaluation, where the object is basically to give a score to the activity being evaluated, and 'formative' evaluation, where the object is to improve it. Guba and Lincoln (1989) argue that there has been a development from a detached, judgemental, 'third-generation' evaluation to an engaged, responsive 'fourth-generation' evaluation, but it might be more accurate to see it as a structural tension: all evaluation will be to some extent detached (since the evaluation is distinct from the activity) and to some extent engaged (since it aims to establish the worth of the activity). The question is how much engagement, and how much detachment, there is in any particular exercise in evaluation, what scope there is for the various participants to shape the activity, and what use the participants make of it.

There is structural tension in the policy process
In the vertical dimension, policy is characterized by clarity of purpose, and the object of evaluation is to ensure that activity is leading to the accomplishment of known purposes. In the horizontal dimension, there is recognition that there is a diversity of players in the game, and therefore scope for divergence over what constitutes worthwhile activity, and hence ambiguity about how it might be evaluated. Since both these elements of the policy process are always present, there is always going to be tension between them. And not all perspectives are equally valid: 'reducing the road toll among young people' commands more support than 'keeping Year 10 occupied and interested', which in turn carries more weight than 'turning young people into car buyers'. This ambiguity, which was important in getting support for the programme in the first place, is challenged by the process of evaluation, which is shaped by the more presentable (and more measurable) goal of reducing the road toll. This may of course be the intention of those who commissioned the evaluation: contesting the impact of these other participants on the programme. But it shows us the importance of recognizing the range of participants in the game, and the effect that this has on evaluation.

Further reading

The perception of policy as a logical succession of stages (the 'policy cycle') was first put forward by May and Wildavsky in 1978 and has provided the 'mainstream' analytic framework for policy texts (e.g. Hogwood and Gunn 1984), even though its inadequacies as either description or analysis are widely noted (see, e.g., Parsons 1995; Sabatier and Jenkins-Smith 1993). A good illustration of the difficulty people have in trying to operationalize this approach is the third edition (1983) of Pressman and Wildavsky's *Implementation*, because the original text has been left intact, and the rethinking of the fundamental questions about policy which came with the second and third editions can be seen in clearly identified and dated chapters. Rossi and Freeman (1993) give a good introduction to evaluation from the vertical perspective, and Guba and Lincoln (1989) offer a 'horizontal' critique (though neither book uses these terms).

6

What Else Is There?

'Policy' conveys the sense that activity is deliberate and purposeful rather than erratic or random. Developing policy in relation to (say) the foreign language skills of young people or the future development of the economy or global climate change is an assertion of competence and rationality: these things will not just happen, but there will be a conscious ordering of activity to bring about outcomes that are in our best interest. In this sense, policy is the counter to randomness or inertia. But it is not the only way of achieving this: terms like 'politics' and 'management' also imply the deliberate imposition of order. In what way is 'policy' a distinctive way of shaping action?

Policy and politics

'Politics' is a concept very close to 'policy', and distinguishing between the two is not easy. In some of the major European languages, the distinction does not exist: *Politik* in German and *politique* in French cover both the English words, and it proved quite difficult to translate 'policy-makers' into Italian (Ostrom and Sabetti 1975: 41). 'Politics', 'policy', 'polity' and 'police' are all derived from *polis*, the city state of ancient Greece, and when the word 'policy' first emerged in English, it tended to refer to the whole pattern of governance, as in Sir Thomas Smith's *The Manner of Government or Policie of the Realm of England* (*c.* 1565). But over time, distinct usages evolved, and as a German political scientist noted, 'policy' came to acquire in English a 'noninstitutional, purely intentional sort of meaning', and to be further distinguished from 'politics' (Heidenheimer 1986: 4). Why this happened is not clear, but it seems to be related to differences in the 'state tradition' in England as against the rest of Europe, and in particular to the development of representative government.

The emergence of elected representatives as the source of legitimate authority raised questions about the relationship between these representatives and the officials of the government, and the distinction between policy and politics helped to answer these questions. In this perspective, representative government means that the legislators determine the direction of government: that is, they decide 'policy'. In the process, they struggle with one another, and appeal for support – from the voters, from fellow legislators, and from outside interests: this is 'politics'. The officials abstain from any part in this struggle, and then implement the policies of the winners in the legislature.

This formulation served to explain and to justify the place of representatives and officials in the process; whether it was a good description was another matter. If politics was seen as a contest over the right to make policy, clearly, one would impact on the other. But since there were two terms, distinctive connotations have developed: for instance, that policy is concerned with outcomes, whereas politics is concerned with process – and in particular, with the participants' position in the game. Policy is seen as detached, but politics is partisan – e.g. doing favours for supporters. The demands of the struggle for advantage ('politics') might be at odds with the pursuit of a desired goal ('policy'). Putting off action on a contentious issue might be 'good politics but bad policy'.

But while we can distinguish between the connotations attached to 'policy' and 'politics', it is difficult to separate them in practice. We recognized that part of the 'horizontal dimension' of policy was the contest between participants. Not only do the various participants have their own distinct perspective on the process, they are (to a greater or lesser extent) in continuing competition with one another. This means that questions like, 'Who are the people proposing this? Do they think like us and tend to support what we do? Will we need their support in the future?' will always be relevant.

So there is always an element of politics in the policy process, but the distinction between politics and policy is drawn on in shaping the action. Special staff may be appointed to ministerial offices to do 'political' work which is deemed inappropriate for permanent officials. It may be, for instance, that the task of mobilizing support in the legislature for a change in agricultural policy has to be given to the 'political' staff, but that it is acceptable for permanent officials to be engaged in mobilizing support among industry groups. The two terms carry different connotations, and there is a strong normative element in the distinction, with 'politics' tending to come off second-best in the comparison.

Policy and administration

The distinction between policy and politics is balanced, in a sense, by the distinction between policy and administration: politics is seen as what leads up to policy, and administration as what flows from it. In this view, the policy process has two stages: first, decisions are taken about the goals to be pursued ('policy') and then people give effect to these decisions ('administration'). This analytic distinction between types of activity is equated with a division of labour among the participants: there are some people whose work is to choose goals ('the policy-makers') and others whose work is to give effect to already-determined goals ('administrators'). In the American literature, it is often the members of the legislature who are seen as the 'policy-makers'. In Westminster-type systems, the policy-makers are assumed to be the ministers, and perhaps the most senior officials as well.

Distinguishing 'administration' from 'policy' in this way reinforces the place of legitimate authority, because it is the people in authority who determine the goals, and officials simply determine how best to accomplish them. Organizations are instruments for the accomplishment of authorized purposes. This presentation of the action also insulates officials from the involvement of the leaders in the detailed work of government: their role is simply to determine the goals; it is for the officials to find the best way to achieve them. This was the primary concern of reformers like Woodrow Wilson, the Professor of Public Administration who went on to become President of the US, who asserted the need to make this clear distinction, and to buttress it with a permanent and non-partisan civil service, in order to get good government: efficient and impartial administration is the implied counterpart of authorized policy (Wilson 1887).

The attraction of this analysis is that it is easy to grasp, and explains a number of things: not only where policy comes from, but also why participants are in the game, and what they do. But as an empirical statement, the explanation looks a little forced. Administration seems to consist of more than simply responding to the choices of authorized leaders. It seems inadequate to say that the officials who are running the public schools or the agricultural extension service or the immigration service are simply giving effect to the prior decisions of ministers or legislators. They are specialists with a commitment to their area of activity, who from time to time need to get the support of these authority figures, but they are not dependent on them for goals. Nor should we assume that all the activity of officials is directed to the achievement of some authorized goal. Empirical observation suggests that these participants are also responding to pressures from their clientele, collecting information, using their specialist skills, and generally keeping the show on the road. In other words, in practice 'administration' cannot be seen as a separate and subordinate sphere of action: we find 'politicians performing administrative duties and administrators assuming political responsibilities' (Caiden 1982: 82). The separation of the two is described as 'a myth' (Hughes 1994: 35).

Why is there this gap between the model and what we see around us? A common explanation is that there has been a shift in practice: once, there was a clear distinction between policy and administration, but in contemporary conditions, this is no longer the case (e.g. Hughes 1994). Or the model may be described as an 'ideal' which is normatively desirable but not attained in practice.

A different explanatory approach is to take the myth seriously: that is, to see it as 'a narrative created and believed by a group of people which diverts attention from a puzzling part of their reality' (Yanow 1996: 191). The presentation of public action in terms of authorized decision and administration to give effect to it answers the problem of where direction comes from in government, and how it may be changed: it comes from the electoral process, and the subordination of officials to authorized representatives; this is 'administration'. This is an account of government which is open to empirical challenge, but as Cuthbertson says (1975: 157), a myth is 'immune to factual attack'. So the account is enunciated by participants on public occasions and recycled in academic accounts. It is often criticized as either an anachronism or an unattainable ideal, whereas in fact it is neither: it is part of the 'sacred', an official account of the policy process, normative rather than empirical, but important as an affirmation of values (see Colebatch and Degeling 1986).

Policy and management

Another concept that is an alternative to policy is 'management', a term which had been associated more with the private sector but is increasingly being applied in public contexts. Some see this as reflecting a substantial change in practice. Hughes, for instance, argues that there has been 'a transformation in the public sectors of advanced countries' which has made the traditional distinction between 'policy' and 'administration' obsolete. While 'public servants carry out policies derived from others ... Instead of merely following instructions, a public manager focuses on achieving *results* and taking responsibility for doing so' (Hughes 1994: 1, 5–6). He cites Allison's exposition of the 'functions of general management': 'strategy' (establishing objectives and devising plans to achieve them), 'managing internal components' (meaning your own staff), and 'managing external constituencies' (other parts of your organization, other organizations, the press and the public), and argues that these functions are now 'routinely carried out by public servants' (ibid.: 62). In this context, 'policy' becomes redundant. Hughes sees 'public policy' as meaning 'policy analysis' and as being 'mainly concerned with the application of formal mathematical methods in the public sector' (ibid.: 145).

Similar claims are made for the 'new public management' (e.g. Osborne and Gaebler 1992), although it is not always clear whether the model presented is a description of what is or has been achieved or advocacy of what could be or should be. This reflects a failure to distinguish clearly between empirical and normative accounts of the world: Hughes's suggestion that 'traditional' public servants had no goals of their own, but were 'simply carrying out the instructions of the politicians' (1994: 61) would not get a great deal of support from the politicians.

But to the extent that the analysis of the 'new public management' is descriptive, it recognizes that public officials are not simply the passive recipients of authorized directions, which was noted in the policy literature in the debate over 'top-down' and 'bottom-up' perspectives. It also recognizes that relations have to be conducted with 'external constituencies', which is what we have been discussing as the 'horizontal dimension' of policy.

It would seem that this approach is a distinct perspective on the same terrain, rather than a description of new territory. It stresses the activities of managers rather than the characteristics of collective action, and is better understood as the rhetoric of the managers than as the analysis of public organization. For instance, Hughes's claim that interest groups 'were once regarded with disdain by the bureaucracy' (ibid: 222) is demonstrably untrue, but is an important element in the validation of the activities of present-day managers. And it is not substantially different from our recognition of the horizontal dimension of policy.

So the increasing visibility of 'management' is essentially a rhetorical shift rather than a transformation of policy. Gunn (1987: 33) argues that there has been a succession of intellectual orientations. In the 1950s, he says, the dominant concern in the study of the public sector was with institutional reform and the term used was 'public administration'. In the 1960s, there was a new interest in planning – 'rationalist exercises in strategic decision-making' – which were associated with the term 'public policy'. In the 1980s, the concern has been to reduce public expenditure and to adopt the methods of the private sector, and the term 'public management has become more common'.

Policy and organization

We keep coming back to the fact that above all else, policy is about organization: 'policy', 'politics' and 'management' are all labels for ways of steering organization, each making its own assumptions about the dynamics of organization – about organization as such, but more particularly, about particular organizations and how they may be steered. This organizational dimension is often not specifically addressed in the writing about policy, except perhaps as a source of imperfection after the event – e.g. the 'problem of implementation'. But the study of policy has been grounded in perceptions of the way organizations work (particularly, but not exclusively, in the public sector), and the gap between the way they do work and the way they should.

This can be seen in the long-running debate over 'rational' versus 'incremental' decision-making. This can be traced back to an article written by Charles Lindblom in which he criticized the idea of decision-making as a comprehensive search for the optimal route to the achievement of known ends. Instead, he argued that in practice means and ends are not separable, analysis is limited rather than comprehensive, policy emerges from a succession of small changes rather than a single clear decision, and the test of a good decision is not so much that it achieves known objectives, but rather that people agree with the process by which it was reached. But, he argued, this method (to which the name 'muddling through' was attached) was as rational and systematic as that based on clearly specified objectives (Lindblom 1959).

This provided the base for a set-piece encounter in policy texts and courses between 'rational' and 'incremental' decision-making, but this did not seem to help either the analysis or the practice of policy very much. Indeed, it was claimed that 'the mainstream position was that while the "rational" model was more preferable as a model of how decisions ought to be taken, the "incremental" model best described the actual practice of decision-making in governments' (Howlett and Ramesh 1995: 137).

Lindblom's argument was framed in behavioural terms, but he was making an organizational point, noting that the argument for comprehensive rationality assumed that the decision-maker was in some way outside the action, inscribing decisions on a *tabula rasa* – a clean sheet, with no limitations implied by existing activities. In fact, the decision-makers are part of the action, starting from some position, and confronting the fact of the activities of other people. They tend to begin with the assumption that what they are doing is worth doing, and to the extent that they contemplate alternatives, to think of ones that are rather like what they are doing now. And where changes are sought, they tend to be ones which will meet with acceptance from the other participants rather than opposition. Lindblom argued that the rational choice approach assumed a single decision-maker, but that in fact there were many participants, each with diverse perspectives and interests, and limited ability to force the others to accept their position, so that the outcome was reached by a process of mutual accommodation – 'partisan mutual adjustment' – rather than by a single-minded choice.

Lindblom's critique was elaborated in a number of books and

articles (see Lindblom 1959, 1965, 1979; Braybrooke and Lindblom 1963; Gregory 1989; Lindblom and Woodhouse 1993; Parsons 1995), and generated a great amount of debate. The debate was not helped by a confusion between analysis and advocacy (see Smith and May 1980), which led to Lindblom being stigmatized as an 'apologist for pluralism', but it was also hindered by the lack of interest in the organizational dimension. It did not, for instance, draw on the political science research into 'policy collectivities' (see Chapter 2) or the 'horizontal dimension' of policy (Chapter 3), or the implications of this perspective for the concept of a rational decision. So it is worth drawing attention to the two significant shifts in analytical focus that Lindblom was introducing into the debate:

- a shift from the desired outcome of policy to the process by which policy is made, and
- a shift from the logic of the system as a whole to the logic of the participants.

Lindblom's contribution expands our focus on the policy process; so too did Graham Allison's study of policy-making during the Cuban missile crisis. In this book, *Essence of Decision* (1971), Allison pointed out that there were three distinct perspectives that could be used to make sense of the action – three different ways of mapping the policy process:

1 *The rational actor.* The action is between identifiable actors – in this case, 'the US' and 'the USSR' – which have clear goals and make choices about the best way to achieve these goals.
2 *The organizational process.* Policy is not made by 'the US' but emerges from the interaction of a range of specialized bodies – e.g. the Pentagon, the CIA, the State Department, the White House – each with its own distinct way of recognizing and dealing with problems.
3 *Bureaucratic politics.* These specialized bodies have different interests and positions, and the policy process is about power relationships and bargaining between them.

As Allison points out, it is not that there are three different sorts of policy-making: all of these elements are part of the total picture. The *'rational actor'* is perhaps the most familiar: there always seems to be an implicit assumption that organizational action *should* be determined by rational choice. This can be traced back to Weber's argument about the process of rationalization in modern industrial society, with factors such as tradition, religion and kinship becoming less persuasive as justifications for action than science, technology and instrumental rationality: we do this in order to achieve some known outcome.

This 'common-sense' assumption was elaborated in the academic discipline of economics, which saw humanity as consisting of separate individuals with clear preferences, who will always choose, from a range of alternatives, the course of action which seems most likely to lead to the accomplishment of their preferences. The policy task, then, is to clarify what the preferences are, to set the policy question up as a choice between alternatives, and to evaluate systematically the relative merits of the alternative ways of achieving these preferences.

The *organizational process* perspective is grounded in empirical observation: although people might talk of organizational goals, organizational activity seems to have more to do with process than with the pursuit and achievement of goals. It is driven more by specialized procedures than by outcomes, and, in this sense, by organizational inertia. This is not to suggest that the organization is doing nothing, but that it is doing what it has always done. Organizations operate through routines: new situations are analysed in terms of past practices. Each organization has Standard Operating Procedures (SOPs) which its members understand and use, and Allison argues that to make sense of the governmental process, we have to understand the SOPs of the various organizational participants. He shows that in the Cuban missile crisis, the differences between the SOPs of the Pentagon, the State Department, the CIA, etc. made a big difference to the way the policy problem was addressed. The implication is that organizations do what they do because it is the appropriate thing to do in that situation, not necessarily in order to achieve some known outcome.

The *bureaucratic politics* perspective recognizes that it is not simply that the different participants have distinct views on the world: they are competitors – for resources, for attention, and for the right to frame the policy question. In order to build its new road, the highways agency must overcome any opposition from the environment protection agency. There is a time dimension, too: the way they deal with one another on any given issue will reflect their experience of previous encounters, and their expectations about the future. In order to advance their concerns, they will need to take note of where they stand in relation to the other participants in the policy process. They will be aware of the positions that other participants are likely to take, and will consider the possibilities of support, alliance and opposition. Even if they do not like the idea of 'playing politics', it will be in their interest to think strategically, otherwise they will simply be the consumers of the strategies of the other participants.

Allison stressed that these should not be seen as three different types of policy process, but three different lenses through which to view the one process. In any policy situation there will be elements of choice (rational actor) and routine (governmental process) and contest (bureaucratic politics), but they will not be the same for all the participants, or at all times, or in all policy fields. Using the three lenses gives us a sharper focus on any given instance of policy activity – whether it is being made or changed or just kept in place.

Some sceptical political scientists argued that this was leaving out of the policy picture the whole question of interest. The central element in the governmental process, they argued, is *constituent benefit*: it is about winning benefits for your side. This analysis could be applied to organizations as such (see Georgiou 1973; Aldrich *et al.* 1994), but is largely applied to 'public politics', and is perhaps best exemplified by Lasswell's classic text, *Politics: Who Gets What, When and How* (1936). This reflects the particular characteristics of the American political system: highly electorally-sensitive, with a powerful rhetoric of popular sovereignty, a very weak sense of state authority, and officials totally dependent for resources on the uncertain approval of the legislature. Legislators facing re-election campaign tirelessly for government spending in their constituencies and, conversely, the activity of government is seen as the embodiment of accumulated particularist demands.

This perspective is not really at odds with Allison's approach – in fact, in some ways, it complements it, recognizing that the participants have an interest in the outcomes. We could add that they also have an interest in the process: for the policy participants, just staying in the game is important. We can link it into the Allison framework via the shift in focus which Lindblom introduced into the debate. We can think of Lindblom's contribution in terms of two cross-cutting dimensions, with Allison's models representing

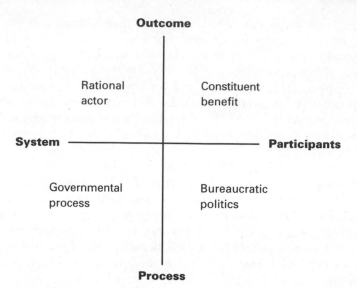

Figure 6.1 Models of the policy process.

ways in which the various elements can be reflected in the policy process.

What this shows is that it all depends on how the map is drawn – both by the participants and by observers. To the extent that people focus on outcomes, and the perspective is that of the system as a whole, it makes sense to think of policy as the work of a rational actor, making choices for society as a whole: 'What sort of child care do we want?' Staying with the system, but thinking more of process than outcome, we think more of framing and specialization and routine: 'How will families and firms and schools and welfare authorities and trade unions respond to the question of childcare?' – i.e. we think in terms of the governmental process. Recognizing that these different bodies are competitors, we would ask: 'How do various participants form an alliance in support of a policy commitment to childcare, and what do the opponents of this commitment (e.g. the Treasury) do to oppose it?' – i.e. we think in terms of bureaucratic politics. And in trying to explain the broad shift in policy, we might argue that with the movement of mothers into the paid workforce, women's groups demanded policy support for childcare (with the implied threat of loss of electoral support if it were not forthcoming) and electorally-sensitive politicians felt obliged to give it – i.e. we are seeing policy as a contest for benefits for constituents.

This example shows that while none of these perspectives gives a complete view of the policy process, all of them have something to contribute, and when used in combination, they give us a much more precise analysis. We can see this if we ask, 'How does each perspective see the central task for policy analysis?'

In the rational actor perspective, the policy task is to choose the best course of action: what should the goal be, and how should it be approached? Elaborate forms of policy analysis have been developed to do this, and separate organizations for 'policy development' or 'policy review' may be created. The 'policy analysis' commonly consists of techniques for identifying alternative courses of action, estimating their likely outcomes, and calculating which alternative best accomplishes known goals (usually expressed in terms of a utilitarian calculus: how much benefit for how many people at what cost?). These calculations yield 'objective' conclusions in support of one particular course of action.

This assumes that organizations exist to pursue goals, these goals are clear, and that the best way to pursue them is a technical matter which can be left to the experts. All of these assumptions are debatable. While it is assumed that organizations have goals, it is not always clear in practice what they are, how they have been chosen, or that organizational activity is best explained as an attempt to achieve these goals. And even if there are clear goals, it is not clear that participants are prepared to accept the judgement of an independent policy analyst about the best way to achieve them: policy inquiry appears to be about interaction and negotiation rather than about scientific detachment.

For these reasons, many observers (and even some practitioners) argue that outcome is less significant than process, and that the focus should be on the continuing practices of the participants rather than proclaimed goals. The driving force in government, they argue, is not the policy preferences of ministers, but the routines of the bureaucracy. Action tends to be framed by functional specialization: roads are the responsibility of a road authority run by road engineers, health is in the hands of a ministry of health run by doctors, education is run by a ministry staffed by teachers, etc. Good work is defined in terms of specialist performance rather than policy outcomes: the focus in (for instance) the water supply agency is on building dams, with less attention being given to whether building another dam is the best answer to the policy problem. Policy documents tend to be statements of current practice, which in turn reflect the particular functional expertise on which the agency is built: 'We do what we're organized to do.'

In this perspective, the policy task is to overcome the inertia of specialist officials. Reformers argued for the establishment of policy units in order both to broaden the way in which policy issues were discussed, and to give ministers more autonomy of specialist officials. These included units located in the agency, but outside the specialist mainstream and reporting directly to the Minister. They might be staffed by people from outside the dominant specialization: the policy unit in health, for instance, might include accountants or social workers in addition to the traditional health professionals. Their distinctive occupational skill would be 'policy'.

But this sort of reform ignores considerations of interest and competitive struggle in the relationships between agencies – that is, of bureaucratic politics. If there is a dispute between the highways agency and the environment protection agency over a new road, it is not simply that the two agencies have different views on the need to conserve the habitats of endangered species. The highways agency is pushing for the endorsement of a major construction project, and the environment protection agency is asserting its right to block the activities of other agencies on environmental grounds. So the policy process involves contest over position in the game, and over the interpretation of the action, which means that the 'adjustment' is likely to be hard-fought, ambiguous and subject to further contest.

The policy task, then, is to find ways to induce the participants to adhere to a common course when the possibility of compelling them to do so is quite small. This task may be pursued through collective bodies (such as 'coordinating committees'), which seek agreement among the participants, or through central policy units aiming to take a 'whole of government' view, such as the Central Policy Review Staff, established in Britain to advise the Cabinet rather than any individual minister. In either case, policy work is a form of diplomacy.

Finally, if we see the policy process as the pursuit of benefits for constituent groups, then policy work has to do with how these claims are made, contested and resolved. If political representatives make claims – for example, for government support for childcare centres – these may be dealt with *ad hoc* ('Can we afford it?' 'Do we need the support of this representative?') But in order to manage these claims over time, the process is likely to become institutionalized – that is, formal channels for handling claims will be established, and rules for dealing with claims will be developed. The organizational channels may initially be quite rudimentary (e.g. using a form, and receiving applications at particular times of the year), but are likely to develop as officials develop specialized expertise, and applicants become more practised and more demanding.

In the same way, the rules may initially be fairly crude and not closely related to needs (e.g., 'The government will meet 50 per cent of establishment costs up to a maximum of $10,000' or, 'The government will only support one centre per representative, per year'), but as the participants become more expert, the rules are likely to become more sophisticated. For instance, the allocation process may take note of the number of working mothers and single parents in the catchment area, the present distribution of centres, the needs of other areas, etc. Cost–benefit analysis, for instance, was developed as a way of dealing systematically with claims on government (see, e.g., Self 1975). There is a close connection between rules and channels: a tribunal staffed by officials trained in economics is likely to frame allocation rules rather differently to a sub-committee of the legislature.

Conclusion

It is clear from this discussion that the relationship between 'policy' and these other terms in common use is not that policy is a new and quite different form of activity, but that it is a distinct way of explaining and shaping the organizational process. This means, of course, that the language is part of the action: the terms that people use – 'policy' or 'management' or 'strategy' – are part of the way in which the participants make sense of what they are doing, justify it and seek support for it. They do this by mobilizing constructs that people share, like 'policy' and 'decision'. The advocates of (for instance) proficiency in languages will seek to establish a 'National Language Policy' as a vehicle for making their case with more moral (and perhaps also legal) force. So the question of whether a matter is 'policy' or 'management' is not simply a technical question, to be resolved by recourse to an authoritative definition: the terms the participants use are part of their repertoire.

We can also see here the continuing tension in organization between the vertical and the horizontal dimension, and the implications that this has for policy. In the vertical dimension, the discussion about policy assumes organizational coherence, hierarchy and instrumentality: what are the organizational goals, and how can they best be attained? In the horizontal dimension, the question is not about *the* organization, but about the range of people and bodies that become relevant for it – the stakeholders, as some call them – and the sort of action that might command support from all or most of them.

Further reading

Parsons (1995: 16–29) gives a good account of the emergence of a distinct 'policy approach' in political science. Wilson's argument (1887) for a clear distinction between policy and administration tends to be cited deferentially, but then dismissed as outdated and unrealistic. Writers like Barrett and Fudge (1981) report that officials are involved in policy-making, and in the US, the 'Blacksburg manifesto' group argued that they should be: that officials have a legitimate and constitutional role (Wamsley *et al.* 1990). On the 'new public management', which to some extent has displaced the interest in policy, see Metcalfe and Richards (1992) and Hughes (1994).

7

Doing Policy

Policy as activity

This series is concerned with concepts in the social sciences, but policy is more than a concept: it is something that people *do*. Even if we avoid (as we have) the assumption that there are clear 'policy-makers', there are people with titles like Policy Analyst and Policy Manager and organizational forms like the Policy Branch, and there are many other people who are working at policy. But what are they doing?

There are several ways of approaching this question: one which focuses on policy as an object, and one whose focus is on policy as a process. The 'common-sense' usage is to see policy as an *object*: there are things called 'policies' – the National Competition Policy, the state planning policy, the school discipline policy – and policy activity means the making of these policies. This implies the exist-ence of a formal statement of the policy, and focuses attention on the activities of the authorized decision-makers (because they make the statement), on the extent to which the stated policy has been carried out (implementation), and to which it achieved its objectives (evaluation).

But many people (including, probably, most practitioners) would say that it is not sufficient just to have a statement of policy. It has to have an impact on what people do, and to achieve this, we have to pay attention to the pattern of action of which the formal state-ment is a part. Policy, they argue, is a *process* which begins long before the formal statement, goes on long after it has been pro-claimed, and may not be accompanied by a formal statement at all.

Even if there is a formal statement, it will not express the complexity of the action. There are many participants, and they all have
varied agendas, so the policy task is to pull them together. Typically,
it goes on over a long period of time, and involves a great deal of
interaction among the participants. In this perspective, doing policy
is not primarily about promulgating formal statements, but about
negotiating with a range of significant participants so that when (or
if) formal statements are made, they accurately reflect what participants have agreed to do, and have a significant impact on what
they actually do.

Of course, the two perspectives are complementary, not contradictory: they are another illustration of the distinction between the
vertical and the horizontal dimension of policy. In the vertical
dimension, the focus is on the authorities making decisions, and
policy activity is seen in terms of 'decision-support' (e.g. identifying and comparing options), checking that decisions have been exe-
cuted and that they have had the desired effect. In the horizontal
dimension, the focus is on the range of participants, the diversity of
their agendas, and the limited capacity to impose a solution by the
use of authorized decisions. Policy activity is seen more in terms of
negotiation, coalition-building, and the ratification of agreed outcomes.

This tension between the vertical and the horizontal perspectives
on policy activity is understood by the practitioners, even if they do
not always give voice to it (remembering, as they do, that what they
say is itself part of the action). The authorized decision-makers
generally recognize that they cannot simply issue commands, but
must in some way deal with people that they cannot command. And
the negotiators operating on the horizontal plane recognize that
their activity must in some way be related to the pattern of authorized decision – e.g. by being described as the 'preparation' of a
policy.

In many ways, our difficulty here is like that which researchers
encountered when they tried to investigate the work of managers.
On the one hand, there was an apparently clear statement of the
role of the manager, which had been appearing in the textbooks
(with only slight variation) since 1916: 'Managers plan, organize,
coordinate and control' (Mintzberg 1971: B97). On the other hand,
when the researchers observed managers in action, little of what
they did could be fitted into these categories. (The researchers were

discovering the vertical and horizontal dimensions of organization in a management context.) They found that managers were engaged in a succession of activities, at great speed, usually initiated by others, and tended to complain of the frantic and unstructured nature of the job. Mintzberg concluded that we should think of the work of the manager not as something which is imposed on the organization from outside, but as an integral part of the process. He suggested that at different times, the manager can be understood as a leader, a nerve centre, a disturbance handler, a resource allocator, etc., as the circumstances demand.

Applying Mintzberg's approach to policy work suggests that we need to be wary of trying to track the making of policy by looking for the policy-makers, i.e. assuming that there are particular systemic tasks to be done and looking around to find who is doing them. Rather, we need to ask what are the things which people do which produce policy: that is, to see policy as a pattern of activity.

The elements of policy activity

For the person trying to map the way policy is made, however, these clarifications seem to become obstacles: if we take both the vertical and the horizontal perspectives into account, (a) there are a great many participants in the policy arena, and (b) it is not always clear what each is contributing to the making of policy.

Certainly, policy is the work of many hands, and it is difficult to know how to take them all into account. Recognizing that policy is activity – it is something that people do – does not mean that all activity is the same, or that it is equally significant. For many of the participants, participation in policy is an occasional activity, sparked by a particular event (like the building of a major road), or a by-product of some other interest. For others, policy is a skilled occupation: they are likely to be engaged in it full-time, and to be paid for it. Sometimes, their policy work will be reflected in their job title (e.g. 'Manager, Policy'); sometimes the title will give no clue (e.g. 'Secretary').

So rather than try to identify particular people as 'policy-makers', it is more fruitful to ask, first, what are the sorts of activity which give rise to policy and, secondly, who are the people who are doing these things, and in what organizational framework? And the best place to start is with the components of policy which we

identified at the outset: authority, expertise and order. What are the
sorts of activity associated with these?

1   *Authority*

The policy process involves the mobilization of authority: ministers
(or Cabinets) make decisions, and legislators pass statutes, and
these people are obviously 'policy actors'. But in each case, there is
a good deal of associated activity. The need for policy to carry authority means that the development of policy has to be channelled to
the source of authority. The minister (and the same applies to
Cabinet or the legislature as the source of authority) may have no
interest in a matter, but it will arrive on his or her desk, and the outcome will be referred to as 'the Minister's decision'. Many people –
officials and organized representatives – are engaged in this chan-
nelling of policy matters to the appropriate authorities (e.g. the
Minister, the Cabinet, the legislature, etc.) In many cases, formal
procedures have emerged: decisions follow written submissions,
which have to be made in specified ways at particular times. There
may be rules for soliciting comments, or (especially in the case of
the legislature) provision for debate. These procedures are in the
custody of specialist officials, such as the staff of the Cabinet Office,
who are very significant 'policy workers', even if they are not always
recognized as such.

2   *Expertise*

The second element of policy activity is the mobilization of relevant
expertise. One of the attributes of a policy field is the existence of a
body of experts – in fact, some would argue that without experts to
identify the problem and propose solutions, there would be no
policy. The emergence of environmental policy, for instance,
depended on the existence of environmental experts. Some of these
were officials in government agencies; others were in universities or
lobby groups or businesses or consulting firms – all engaged in
being expert.

Alongside this expert activity in particular fields emerged what
we could call an 'expertise of choice': a technology for identifying
policy options and choosing systematically between them, which is
usually called 'policy analysis' (though there is also a lot of other

activity claiming that title). In essence, this is a utilitarian calculus: state the objective of the policy, identify alternative ways of pursuing this, estimate the likely costs and benefits of each, and work out the most cost–effective option. More complex versions seek to identify the benefits for each of the affected parties, or to build in estimates of the 'implementability' of the proposal. This sort of analysis is closely linked to evaluation – in fact, it is really an attempt to do the evaluation before the event – and shares its aspiration to transform choice into a form of expert activity.

3   Order

Finally, policy involves the creation of order – that is, shared understandings about how the various participants will act in particular circumstances. 'This is the policy', implies, 'This is how it will be done'. But there are many participants in the field, and many different perspectives on the situation and the task, so these shared understandings have to be created. This is not simply an intellectual exercise. Understandings express values and interests, not simply abstract knowledge. The emergence of policy on the environment was not simply the result of policy participants acquiring new knowledge, but also of a shift in the way people valued things – industrial production and jobs, for instance, as compared to clean air and rivers. So creating order involves dealing with values. It also involves questions of organization. Different organizations have their characteristic perspectives on the policy field, and creating order may challenge the assumptions and working practices of the organizations involved, and will demand interaction between organizations, and possibly lead to organizational change.

Types of policy activity

We have clarified what is involved in the activity of policy, but this does not identify distinct types of policy activity – some concerned with authority, others concerned with expertise, etc. – because the elements are intertwined with one another. Expertise is mobilized in the service of order: e.g. an inter-organizational task force on increasing river pollution calls in scientific consultants to help them find a policy response that all of them can accept. The elements

impact on one another. Expertise builds authority: the pronounce-
ments of the National Health and Medical Research Council on the
health risks of smoking carry more weight than a resolution of the
legislature. Conversely, authority can build expertise: creating an
agency for environmental protection facilitates the development of
environmental policy as a field of expertise. The practice of any participant is likely to involve more than one of the elements. So we
cannot use this analytic clarification to sort the policy participants
into categories, but it does help us to clarify the differences between
the sorts of policy activity in which the various participants are
engaged. It helps to think of them in terms of some fairly broad
general types: leaders, aides, followers, executives, maintenance
staff, interested parties and knowledge workers.

1   Leaders

Some people are policy participants by virtue of their standing in
the process of representative government. They may have been
elected to the legislature; in countries with a Westminster system,
they may have become ministers; in other systems, they may have
been appointed to a leadership position by the people who won the
election. In any case, they hold their position by virtue of demonstrated public support, and may lose it if that support fades. The
same can be said (though it is less marked) of leaders in non-
government organizations.

We could expect these leaders to be particularly active in the
policy field since, as we noted at the beginning, candidates for
public office are expected to declare policies on a wide range of
issues, and the outcome of the election is held to be a popular
endorsement of the policies of the winners: it is said to give them a
'mandate' to implement these policies.

This sets up one sort of policy activity: exercising the authority
of office to impose an electorally endorsed course of action on a
(perhaps reluctant) governmental machine. There is a clear policy:
the task is to implement it. The leader and his or her staff will be
active in declaring what the policy is, and looking for confirmation
that it is being carried out. They will be able to insist on the priority
of their policy because of the authority of the election and their
position of leadership. And they will be monitored by the press,
which is interested in critically reviewing the performance of

government in the light of the policy undertakings given at the last election.

This sort of policy activity can certainly be seen, but there are clearly other forces at work. The election platform was drafted at a particular point in time: it is likely that the situation will have changed in relation to the things that were included in the platform, and that new issues have arisen. In any case, the platform was probably expressed in fairly non-specific and ambiguous terms, in order to appeal to as many people, and alienate as few, as possible.

Moreover, the leader is now responsible for the continuing programmes of the agency, as well as the undertakings in the platform. And she or he is also concerned about the maintenance of support, thinking about the next election as well as the last one, and also about the constant contest for influence within the leadership.

This means that there is a built-in tension between programme and process, and leaders will respond to it in different ways. Some may have their eyes fixed firmly on the programme on which they came to office: 'Are we doing what we promised?' Others may be more interested in the process: 'How are we doing in the opinion polls?' 'Will we win the next election?' 'Are we maintaining our influence relative to other agencies?' No leader can completely ignore either aspect, but leaders will respond to this tension in different ways, reflecting their own experience and characteristics, recent policy history and the nature of the interest in this policy field.

2 Aides

An important change in the practice of government in recent years has been the much greater part played by aides to the leaders (minister, legislators, etc.) By this we mean people recruited (often on a temporary basis) to serve the leader personally, and who can expect to lose their jobs if the leader changes, or loses confidence in them. One Australian study, influenced by the well-known British television series, called them 'the Minister's minders' (Walter 1986).

These people are particularly active in policy work, but since their role is relatively new and unstructured, they do it in a variety of ways. They come from a variety of backgrounds. Some may be recruited on the basis of their expert knowledge, e.g. a new Minister for Housing seeking to recruit an aide with specialist knowledge of housing to be an alternative to the department as a source of expert advice. Or they may come from a lobby group, and be recruited to strengthen order by maintaining good relations with organized interests.

Aides are likely to have a particular concern for ideology, and relate party programme issues to the work of government. In this, they experience the tension between programme and process: they are particularly committed to the programme, but the best way to support it is to involve themselves in the process; the more they become involved in the process however, the less forcefully they can assert the programme. Aides who are experts are also drawn into the process. They are unlikely to be left in isolation writing expert opinions, but will need to become involved in a succession of *ad hoc* activities – 'trouble-shooting'. Aides are likely to be particularly concerned with order, and with ensuring that the actions of other participants do not impact adversely on their own leader. They tend to see themselves as 'streetwise', drawing on their own intuition more than on expert knowledge.

3   Followers

To talk of leaders implies followers, yet they tend to be forgotten in discussions about policy. Backbench legislators in Westminster systems are often dismissed as 'lobby fodder', controlled by the party whips. But their continuing support is vital for the leaders, and it is possible for it to be withdrawn. Individual followers are likely to complain that it is difficult for them to exercise a significant role in the making of policy but, collectively, the followers are a significant negative force. If the followers are sufficiently determined in the party room, they can compel the leaders to modify or withdraw unpopular policies. In this way, they act collectively to set the parameters of action by the leaders, who must always ask themselves, 'Will the followers wear this?'

4   Executives

By this we mean the top management level in the organizations over which the leaders preside. Traditionally, this has been seen as distinct from, and subordinate to, the level at which policy is determined: policy is determined by leaders, and implemented by executives. A century ago, Woodrow Wilson argued strongly for the separation between policy and administration, which he saw as necessary to ensure that responsibility for policy rested with the elected leaders, and that career officials followed the instructions of the elected leaders. The same distinction was made in Westminster systems: ministers made policy and were responsible to Parliament for it, and officials implemented the policies of whichever government was in power, irrespective of their own preferences.

This was a normative model of the governmental process rather than an empirical one: it stated the proper relationship between ministers and their officials, rather than described the actual relationship. But it created the terminology for talking about the policy process at this level. It is now argued that 'a new model of public management has effectively supplanted the traditional model of public administration' (Hughes 1994: 59), and that managers are now responsible for 'strategy', entailing 'the future of the organization, establishing objectives and priorities and making plans to achieve these' (ibid: 61), which does not seem to leave much room for policy.

This new model of public management, like the model which it supplants, is normative rather than empirical: the literature contains more exhortation and prediction than description. The new-model public sector manager would, of course, be in the same position as the managers studied by Mintzberg: while the model depicts the manager as making and applying plans with cool detachment, the experience of the process is a kaleidoscopic succession of brief but intense episodes, largely generated by others, which does not look much like planning. But the model generates the language and the expectations: top management is expected to plan the direction of organizational activity, and not to wait for directions from the elected leaders. Managers are expected to take an active role in developing policy. They may do this by initiating the preparation of policy statements – that is, systematic, intention-driven portraits of their organization's activities – and presenting them for endorsement by the leaders. Practice within the organization is likely to be described in policy terms: the policy on recycling, the policy on quality improvement, the policy on smoking in the workplace.

Seeing policy development as a managerial task frames policy in terms of the application of authority, and focuses attention on the

vertical dimension: it is something that happens within the organization. But most policy activity has a horizontal dimension, and
involves the activities of other organizations – business, voluntary
groups, and other levels of government. Policy on youth unemployment will involve not only the labour department, but also the
agencies responsible for education, social services and youth
affairs, unions, business groups and community bodies. It is not
simply a matter of what the manager can achieve with his or her
own resources, but this aspect gets less attention in the 'new public
management' model.

5   Maintenance staff

What the example of youth unemployment policy reminds us of is
that a great deal of policy activity consists of building up and sus-
taining working relationships among different organizations (or
distinct units within the same organization), and activity which predominantly falls to middle-level officials who can be thought of as
the 'maintenance staff' of the policy process. These officials are apt
to remark that the most important attribute for a policy worker is
neither expertise nor authority, but patience: they spend their time
trying to make the activities of the various participants compatible
with one another, in situations where different authorities are operating, and there is no agreement on the best answer.

This involves a great deal of interaction among the interested
parties, ranging from individual telephone calls and informal chat
at semi-social occasions to public meetings and formal negotiations.
There are many organized forums for this interaction, ranging from '
permanent committees to *ad hoc* working parties, and recognized
processes of consultation – e.g. inviting interested parties to
comment on the drafts of statements or other official documents.
The object of this activity is to communicate to the other participants the policy perspective of the organization, to discover what
their perspective is, to identify where the positions of the participants are in conflict, and to seek paths to agreement. This may focus
on the preparation of a new policy statement, or it may be concerned with the implications of existing policies – for instance, on
the implications for local health authorities of central government
policies on appropriate care for ex-servicemen.

In the process, the participants draw on the expert knowledge they have (or have acquired) of the policy subject matter – education, agriculture, forestry, etc. But they also draw on their detailed knowledge of the policy field: what has been done previously, which participants are involved, what they consider to be the important questions,what stances they have taken on key issues in the past, what commitments limit their freedom of action now, etc. This knowledge helps them find ways to knit together the diverse activities in a way which the different participants can accept: in this respect, 'making policy' is more like diplomacy than architecture.

But what place does this leave for the systematic identification of policy options and the assessment of their relative utility – 'policy analysis', as many people would understand it? There is a large literature in this sort of analysis, grounded in microeconomics, established educational programmes, and many officials with the title 'Policy Analyst'. Certainly, the identification and comparison of options has a respectable place in the policy process. For the maintenance workers, though, this sort of analysis is not conclusive in itself. It is useful, in that it clarifies what is at stake for the organization, it informs the actions of the maintenance staff, and it may yield information which can form part of the negotiating process. But its importance lies in the way in which it can be used in this continuing process: the analysis will not settle the question on its own.

6   *Interested parties*

We have seen that there are many players in the policy arena, and that they include 'outsiders' as well as public officials. In each field of policy, there will be a number of people who have an interest in the area, and they tend to be a relatively well-known cast of players. Organizations emerge to represent interests: in education policy, there are bodies to represent parents, teachers, disciplinary fields, employers, educators, and a variety of groups wanting to see their particular concerns – foreign languages, citizenship, international affairs, driving, drugs – better reflected in the curriculum. The policy process tends to draw organized interests into a stable relationship with the official players through recognized processes of consultation, and officials facilitate the recognition of representative groups: in this way, they organize their clientele. In doing this, they shape the way the policy question is understood and the interests that are recognized: some interests are organized in, and some are organized out.

The interest representatives themselves generally want to be on the inside but, once they get there, they are faced with a tension between asserting the viewpoint of their constituents, and becoming involved in the detail of the policy process. Their claim to a place in the action is based on their knowledge of what their constituents want but, in the policy process, these wants have to be related to all the other relevant factors, and the representatives may become involved in trading off the demands of their own constituents in the search for an agreed outcome.

In some ways, this is no more than happens to any negotiating representative but, in the policy case, there is a time dimension. Over time, the participants are drawn into the game, and both officials and the representatives of organized interests are engaged in the same sort of activity: an informed search for a workable and acceptable outcome. Representation becomes institutionalized and professionalized. Initially, it will be done by enthusiastic amateurs; as the organization becomes established, it engages paid, expert staff, who can be more effective in the detailed work. The homelessness action group hires staff with qualifications in sociology and economics, who can talk to the policy professionals on their own terms. Governments facilitate the process by encouraging (often subsidizing) the formation of peak organizations, which both brings together small groups into one organization and raises the level of professional expertise in interest representation. Policy activity is concentrated on the negotiations among a knowledgeable group, 'camped permanently around each source of problems', as Davies put it, who share both a field of concern and a body of expert knowledge about it. This is a potential source of conflict with these interest organizations, a structural tension between authenticity and effectiveness: only the members can say how they really feel, but hiring the experts will give them a more effective voice in policy.

7   Knowledge workers

As well as the various office-holders whose activities we have been discussing, there are also those whose participation in the policy process comes not so much from the position they hold, but from the specialist knowledge they have: we can call them 'knowledge workers'. They play an important policy role because of their influence in shaping the terms of the debate: what is regarded as normal, what is a problem, and what possible answers to the problem are there?

In agricultural policy, for instance, there are academics in such fields as agricultural science, plant biology and agricultural economics. There are also agricultural experts working for banks, trading companies, professional bodies, consulting firms, or as private consultants. There are journalists working for the press and for specialist industry-oriented journals. All of them are part of a specialist discourse about agriculture, and potential participants in the discussion of agricultural policy.

They may have no formal standing in the process, but their contribution can be very important, particularly in the medium to long term, as the terms of the policy debate shift. Such changes often reflect changes in the environment, but they also stem from changes in the terms of the debate among the knowledge workers, which in turn reflects debate in the broader society. For instance, in the 1980s, the discourse on agricultural policy shifted from an assumption that, ultimately, farming should be protected to an assumption that, essentially, market forces should operate, and this shift (which reflected the broader debate about the role of the state) could also be seen in the positions taken by organized interests in the industry. Despite the gloomy assumption of many knowledge workers that their research has little impact on policy, it was clear that, over time, there was a fundamental change in the basic understanding on which policy rested.

Policy activity and policy-making

The study of policy is already overloaded with fine terminological distinctions, and the reader may ask why we have avoided the familiar term 'policy-making', and introduced a new term 'policy activity'.

The most obvious reason is that it is clear that there is a great deal of activity, and that it is not well-described as policy-*making*, in the sense which the textbook model implies: the deliberate choice of a preferred outcome by an authorized decision-maker. Most of what happens is neither as crisp nor as final as that. The authorized decision-maker becomes one of a number of participants, and many of these are responsible to other authority figures, so 'what the government wants' becomes problematic: the question becomes, 'How do people produce the outcomes which are described as the decisions of the government?' It becomes difficult to distinguish one of these participants as the person 'making' the policy. Even if we can identify one person as the prime mover, and even if that person is the authorized leader, it is rarely the case that they can make the policy on their own: there are others whose advice or consent is needed.

Linked to this is the evident importance of 'non-officials' in policy. People who are neither authorized leaders nor their officials are active at putting matters on policy agendas, framing the problem, canvassing solutions, and giving effect to the outcome. Environmental policy, for instance, reflects not so much the intentions of the government in relation to the environment as the success of environmental activists and others at making this an issue on which governments have to take a stance, mobilizing public opinion and electoral support, and establishing the terms of the debate. But it would hardly seem appropriate to describe them as 'making policy'.

Finally, talking about policy activity directs our attention first to the process, and only secondly to the outcome, particularly when the outcome is seen as a formal statement. Much policy work is only distantly connected to authorized statements about goals: it is concerned with relating the activities of different bodies to one another, with stabilizing practice and expectations across organizations, and with responding to challenge, contest and uncertainty. It may be that statements by authorized leaders about goals are brought into play, but there will be a great deal of other activity as well, and it is important that the terms we use do not give an undue prominence to one part of the game.

Further reading

Perhaps surprisingly, there is less written about what policy participants actually do than on almost any other aspect of policy. Leaders often write their memoirs, and these sometimes offer valuable insights into the policy process (see, e.g. Crossman 1975), but followers, aides and maintenance workers rarely do, though studies like Bardach's *The Implementation Game* (1977) and Meltsner's *Policy Analysts in the Bureaucracy* (1976) are a useful source, as is Walter's *The Minister's Minders* (1986).

8

Policy as a Concept and as Practice

The meaning of policy

One might have expected this section to come at the beginning of the book rather than at the end, but as we saw from the outset, the term is used in a variety of ways, and it was more fruitful to leave them all on the table while we explored what they had to offer. The concern of this book has been in the way that the concept is used, rather than in defining one particular use as 'correct'. But it is now appropriate to come back to the question of the meaning of the concept, and the relationship between the concept of policy and the practice of policy.

The fact that the term is used in so many ways is itself a source of concern to some. 'Students of government', says Hughes, 'have long struggled over what is meant by "policy" and "policy-making"', leading him to conclude that '[i]t is not possible to define public policy in any precise way' (1994: 146). The unnoticed equation of 'policy' with 'public policy' does, however, significantly limit the field of vision, and some writers would like to confine the term to governmental decision-making. 'Public policy is, at its most simple, a choice made by a government to undertake some course of action', assert Howlett and Ramesh (1995: 5). But this still defines the term fairly broadly.

> One popular text on policymaking defines policy as 'whatever governments choose to do or not to do' (Dye 1985: 1). (This recalls Mark Twain's description of the River Platte: 'a mile wide and an inch deep'.) Other texts make similarly expansive claims. 'Policy refers both to intentions and to actual results' (Gordon 1978: 355). What, then, was our policy in Vietnam?
>
> (Hale 1988: 436)

The term 'government' is itself a problem, since the people involved in the making of policy are not quite the same as 'the government'. Some are 'governmental', but they are not necessarily all pushing the same way, and some appear to be 'non-governmental'. This uncertainty about who the actors are is reflected in some of the definitions. Jenkins, for instance, sees public policy as 'a set of interrelated decisions taken by a political actor or group of actors concerning the selection of goals and the means of achieving them within a specified situation where those decisions should, in principle, be within the power of those actors to achieve' (Jenkins 1978: 15).

Some writers feel that definitional questions just get in the way:

> In short, the debate about definitions has largely dissipated without result? [*sic*] Australian academics, pragmatic to the end, gave up the endless definitional jostling to get on with substantive policy work. Public policy as analysis shares with public policy as practice a range of methods and levels. It does not matter what disciplinary boundaries seem appropriate, since governments go on making (and remaking) decisions regardless.
>
> (Davis *et al*. 1993: 10)

Here, policy consists of 'governments making decisions': no further clarification is seen as necessary. But the question is what sort of practice this label denotes: what happens when 'governments make decisions'?

The source of the difficulty in reaching a satisfactory definition is that there are, both in the academic literature and in the working knowledge of practitioners, two fundamentally different perspectives on policy: one about *authorized choice*, and one about *structured interaction*.

The *authorized choice* perspective assumes that policy is indeed about 'governments making decisions', and focuses on such decisions. It asks questions about the problem that the government was trying to address, the options with which it was presented, how it made the choice it did, and what the outcome was: did the policy chosen solve the problem being addressed?

The *structured interaction* perspective does not assume a single decision-maker, addressing a clear policy problem: it focuses on the range of participants in the game, the diversity of their understandings of the situation and the problem, the ways in which they interact with one another, and the outcomes of this interaction. It does not assume that this pattern of activity is a collective effort to achieve known and shared goals.

These two perspectives frame the action in divergent ways, and both practitioners and observers have to work out how to accommodate the divergence between them. People respond to this divergence in different ways.

1   A reform agenda

This divergence between ideal and practice gives rise to a reform agenda: the goal of reform should be to make 'authorized choice' the practice, and not just a theoretical ideal. Deborah Stone calls this 'the rationality project': the mission 'of rescuing public policy from the irrationalities and indignities of politics, hoping to conduct it instead with rational, analytical and scientific methods' (Stone 1988: 4). This is a sentiment which underlies much of the enthusiasm for policy and policy units and policy analysis: if systematic analysis could be brought to bear on the problem, the most efficient course of action would be evident, and because it had emerged from this analysis, it would command widespread support.

In this context, the focus on policy is a reform move: paying attention to outcomes rather than process, and making choices in order to accomplish priority goals rather than because of habit, political pressure or technological inertia. It was hoped that central policy review agencies in government, not being committed to existing programmes, would be better placed to review their contribution to the achievement of policy goals, and similar hopes were held of policy units in organizations.

This systematic linking of policies, needs and outcomes should also, it was felt, flow through the workings of government generally, which must be understood as an instrument for the accomplishment of policy objectives.

> The use of the term 'program' reflects the value now placed on the coherent organization of government activities into 'programs' of closely related components all of which are, or ought to be, managed according to the policy priorities established under the formal authority of the program objectives . . . evaluation is the current phase of that deliberate pursuit of rational public management which

originated in the struggles for program budgeting and management by
objectives.

(Uhr and Mackay 1992: 433)

2   *Theory and practice*

Another common response, especially amongst practitioners, is to
describe the 'authorized choice' perspective as 'theory' and the
'structured interaction' perspective as 'practice'. For example, 'In
theory, policy is made by government making a clear choice of the
most effective response to a known problem, but in practice it
emerges from struggles between powerful interests pursuing different agendas and is marked by contest and uncertainty.'

Here, 'theory' is being used not in the sense of an abstract explanation of the way the world works, but in a more normative way:
this is the way that the world should work, but does not. In an ideal
world, governments would single-mindedly begin with the problem
and work out the best solution, but in practice, there are many
voices in government, and they all view the problem from the perspective of what they are doing themselves, and how to turn the
policy-making to their advantage. The 'authorized choice' perspective is seen as an ideal which people respect but are not necessarily
expected always to follow.

This perspective sees the competing perspectives as different
kinds of knowledge: practitioners and observers know different
sorts of things. Schmidt points out that different sorts of workers
know quite different things about the same project. The engineers
who designed the dam have a detailed knowledge about it derived
from their professional training and their knowledge of the design;
the workers at the dam wall have a different sort of knowledge,
based on shared experience and intuition: 'a feel for the hole' (see
Schmidt 1993). In the same way, the knowledge that policy workers
have about the policy process – about position and negotiation and
compromise and commitment – seems of a different kind to that
implied in academic writing about problem-solving and the policy
cycle. They respect the trappings of authorized choice – the systematic study of needs, the ordering of options, the calculation of
costs and benefits – but it is seen as being somewhat remote from
the 'real world'.

3 An analytic tool

For some writers, the divergence between the two perspectives is not a problem. Analytic constructs in the social sciences, they would argue, are not descriptions of empirical cases, and differences between models and practice are neither surprising nor disturbing. For such writers, the development of a model of policy as authorized choice can help us to understand the policy process, even though the process does not resemble the model. Howlett and Ramesh, for instance, develop a model of policy as a cycle of applied problem-solving:

- agenda-setting
- policy formulation
- decision-making
- policy implementation
- policy evaluation.

They argue that 'this facilitates the understanding of public policy-making by breaking the complexity of the process into a limited number of stages and sub-stages', though they stress that the practice of policy does not follow the model – decision-makers do not act in a systematic way, the stages may occur in a different order or be omitted entirely, there may be a series of small loops rather than one big one – 'In short, there is often no linear progression as conceived by the model' (1995: 12).

But although the model bears little resemblance to the experience of policy, they assert that if the model is further developed by being made more elaborate – e.g. by developing a taxonomy of policy styles – 'such a model contributes to the development of a policy science by providing a much better understanding of why governments choose to do what they do or do not do' (p. 14). It is not clear, though, how a model which diverges so markedly from practice can offer a better understanding of practice.

4 An organizational construct

The argument in this book has been that policy emerges from an organizationally-complex process in which the formal model plays an important part. More specifically, we have argued as follows.

(i) Policy has a horizontal and a vertical dimension
The vertical dimension is concerned with authoritative decision-making: as Dye and others would put it, 'Policy is what governments decide to do.' This focuses attention on 'the authorities', and defines their activity as 'making policy'. It also defines the activities of the other participants: they are either engaged in 'policy advice' (before the event) or 'policy implementation' (after it). Lines of authority are important in the vertical dimension: 'policy' is an assertion of authority over practice, limiting the autonomy of both officials and clients. It is important that officials be autonomous of outside influences and not be 'captured' – e.g. that those concerned with environmental policy might end up as the voice of environmental interests within the government, rather than the instrument of the government.

The vertical dimension also directs attention to the goals of the policy-makers: policy is 'a purposive course of action' (Anderson 1984: 3), or as Howlett and Ramesh put it, an exercise in 'applied problem-solving' (1995: 11). This provides the logical link to policy evaluation – 'Have the purposes been accomplished? Has the problem been solved?' – which then feeds into a new round of decision-making by 'the government'. And because it directs attention to goals, it acts as an inducement to organizations to enunciate objectives, and to attach weight to them – e.g. by linking the pay of senior staff to the accomplishment of defined objectives.

This is a neat and logical presentation of the policy process, concerned with relationships within the organization, reflecting its assumption that this is where policy is carried out. But policy practitioners find that much of their time is taken up with dealings with people outside their own organizational unit: in other units in the same organization, in other organizations, or in no organization at all. In any policy field, there will be a wide range of interested parties – governmental, semi-governmental, and not governmental at all – who will be involved for different reasons, and see the question in different ways. Any policy question is likely to involve a number of organizations, with differing understandings of the question, and varying degrees of interest in cooperating with other bodies.

The outcome will be a pattern of interaction between participants engaged in different projects, rather than the pursuit of clear and shared objectives. The interaction will not be random, as the policy process operates to turn conflict and participation into routinized activities. But it will probably not be neat or smooth: there is likely to be overlap and conflict, and the policy process will be concerned with negotiation and ambiguity rather than decision and order, with identifying who is interested, and from what perspective, in order to reduce uncertainty and make the policy issue more manageable.

(ii) Policy is about linkage as much as problem-solving
The policy process is about the knitting-together of the participants, which requires a number of things:

- *Time* – not just in the sense that one needs time today to pursue these questions, but also in the sense that the longer a policy field has been recognized as such, the more likely the participants are to have become accustomed to one another and to find it easier to work together.
- A degree of shared *understanding* of the policy field. Participants come from different directions, and what they know is often in conflict with what other participants know. Working together helps to develop knowledge that they have in common: it is an exercise in policy learning, not simply interpersonal acquaintance.
- *Organizational settings* where this learning can take place – whether they are specifically established for this purpose, like the advisory bodies established within the public sector to bring together the diverse interests in the policy field, or whether they simply operate in this way, like industry conferences or even agricultural shows.
- *Functional specialization* can help the development of this horizontal organizing and learning. Government specialists in a particular field (e.g. industrial safety) will have more in common with people from other organizations who are working in this field than with people from their own organization working in another field, such as union registration or labour market trends. They will learn where these people are located, and will consult them in order to generate support for policy moves that they may want to make.
- *Participants come from inside and outside government.* For instance, a policy response to the question of appropriate

education for children with disabilities will involve 'the government', but not as a single-minded individual. There will be
demands from various therapists, parents and disability lobby
groups, reflected in discussions and proposals in health, welfare
and educational organizations, negotiations among officials and
perhaps ministers. The outcome may be agreement on a course of
action which is endorsed by the Cabinet, and is then announced as
'the decision of the government', but which reflects the actions and
preferences of the officials and advocates concerned with children
with disabilities more than it does problem-solving by ministers.

(iii)   The rational model has symbolic importance

Framing the process as problem-solving through authoritative
rational choice is an important part of making the outcome acceptable: policy has force because it has been generated in a proper way.
We live in a secular industrial society which believes in technology
and rationality, and it calls for a technology of rational choice. As
March and Olsen put it, 'It is hard to imagine a society with modern
Western ideology that would not require a well-elaborated and
reinforced myth of intentional choice through politics, both to sustain a semblance of social orderliness and meaning and to facilitate
change' (March and Olsen 1989: 52).

So the vertical perspective, in which policy is presented in terms
of the pursuit of authorized goals, becomes an essential part of its
validity.

> The ritual of identifying what their goals are and discussing them at
> the annual meeting was conveying to members and stakeholders that
> the organization is a modern, rational organization and that it is doing
> its work properly, even if it is difficult to demonstrate accomplishment
> of these goals.
>
> (Yanow 1996: 201)

(iv)   The model frames appropriate behaviour

It defines the role of elected executives – ministers, for instance, or
municipal councillors – in terms of the determination of goals, and
that of other officials as carrying these out. This becomes an explanation of this relationship, which meets the needs of both participants and observers, even if it is not a good description of what the
participants do. In this context, the concept of policy is a part of the
invocation of ministerial authority: both the minister and the

officials are mobilizing the concept of policy as authorized and rational decision-making to validate what they do.

It also validates the activities of other participants: e.g. if schools are to punish students, they should have a 'discipline policy'. The counter official who says, 'The policy of this department is only to respond to complaints that are submitted in writing' is invoking the concept of policy to fend off the complainant on the other side of the counter. This policy may not appear in any written document, but when practice is described as policy, it has more force: 'I am not making a judgement about your case, I am simply following policy.'

The mobilization of the concept of policy is also an assertion of central control: the focus on the goal upholds the power of the authorities against the claims of clients or local interests or even the inertia of the organization. Policy units seek to identify and compare alternative policy objectives, and evaluation teams assess whether the desired objectives have been achieved. It has become common for senior executives in government to be placed on 'performance-based' contracts, with remuneration being tied to the achievement of specified outcomes.

(v)   The framing is predominantly vertical

The concept of policy which the participants mobilize is dominated by the vertical dimension, with its stress on authorized choice, known goals and clear outcomes, but functional specialization means that the policy concept has to be broadened to take in the horizontal: if the government has separate departments for health, welfare and education, then policy on the immunization of young children will involve a number of organizations which may well have different views on whether and how to proceed.

The horizontal dimension has received more explicit recognition in the development of the concept of 'stakeholders', people or organizations who had an interest in what the organization did and who are entitled to be heard and to be taken seriously. But this still carries less weight than the vertical: in the public presentation, it is for the authorized leaders to decide how much voice the stakeholders should have.

(vi)   This means ambiguity about decision-making

Recognizing the claims of stakeholders qualifies the notion of policy emerging from decisions by authorized leaders, and in

recognizing the 'horizontal' claims of stakeholders, policy practitioners are careful to do it in a way which leaves intact the concept
of authoritative decision. Referring to the process as 'advising' preserves the position of the minister as the person making the choice.
The public inquiry also provides an opportunity for stakeholders to
negotiate policy change which can then be announced by the minister.

This shows us the way in which the model contributes to shaping
the process. An outcome which has been negotiated among interested parties is set in place by being announced by the voice of authority – the Minister, the Cabinet, the legislature. The production of
this policy outcome is the work of many participants, but it is publicly presented as a choice by one point of authority. Having been
constructed, it must be (as Weick 1979 puts it) 'enacted': the form
of the presentation is part of the process. 'Everyone knows' that
what is announced as a ministerial decision probably reflects a
complex process of inter-organizational negotiation more than it
does the preferences of that particular minister, but it is inappropriate to point this out: this is part of the 'profane' knowledge of
the participants, and is not to be stated in the 'sacred' discourse of
public announcements (see Colebatch and Degeling 1986). Authorized decision-making is an essential 'policy myth' in the sense
described by Yanow: 'a narrative created and believed by a group
of people which diverts attention from a puzzling part of their
reality' (Yanow 1996: 191).

Further reading

Parsons (1995: 176–83) offers a useful introduction to the debate
about the symbolic function of policy, to which Edelman (1988) has
been a major contributor. Yanow (1996) is a very informative study
which applies sophisticated theoretical questions to an empirical
case; Schön and Rein's work on framing (1994) is also relevant
here.

9

In Conclusion

Policy has proved an elusive concept, perhaps partly because it is used by practitioners (for whom ambiguity about definitions can be useful) as much as it is by social scientists. The approach in this book has been to avoid imposing a definitional clarity where this might prevent our seeing important elements of the meanings which the term carries. We have seen that it has been difficult to establish a satisfactory definition of policy because there is a model in use which is not a good description, but which is difficult to get away from simply because it is in use. This suggests that a satisfactory definition would have to recognize the tension between the model and the way it is used – e.g., 'Policy is a term used to refer to the structuring of collective action by the mobilization of a model of government as authorized decision-making.' This is an awkward approach to a definition, but it does focus attention on the essential elements. It is worth elaborating on these.

Policy is a process as well as an artefact

In the 'common-sense' use of the term, policy is an artefact: a thing created by 'policy-makers'. We read, for instance, that 'the government has announced its new policy on Equal Employment Opportunity'; some would insist that there must be not only a press statement, but also a statute which expresses the policy. We have argued that these examples of formal policy activity can only be understood in terms of process, a continuing pattern of events and understanding which is structured by a sense of authorized decision-making. For instance, a demand for a population policy is built on a shared perception of the possibility of the conscious use of governmental authority to change the population pattern. The policy process encompasses all the action which takes place around the possibility of this use of governmental authority to structure action, and policy statements – like White Papers or ministerial speeches – are part of this process of structuring.

Some would argue that this turns the whole of the policy world into a blur: there are (they would argue) clear policies – the environment policy, the industry protection policy, the competition policy – and they need to be distinguished from the ordinary process of government. Moreover, they have objectives – the vocational education policy aims to raise the skills level in the workforce, the child immunization policy aims to reduce the level of communicable diseases among children – and we can therefore ask whether or not they 'work'. This is certainly a valid perspective, but it is an incomplete one. These formally stated policies have to be understood in the context of other stated policies – e.g. on the loosening of regulatory controls over the workforce – and of the broader factors that structure action, such as the level of knowledge in government about skill needs in the workforce and the existence of organized links between industry, workers, trainers and government. Statements are important, but they must be understood in context. And as we saw from the discussion of evaluation, whether a programme has 'worked' depends on how the question is framed and who is asked: that, too, is also about process.

But if we are concerned with policy as process rather than simply as formal acts by authorized decision-makers, we have to ask if the structuring without reference to authorized decision-makers should also be considered policy. As we saw, writers like Dearlove held that policy statements are not important: what counts is the commitment of valuable resources, and in some studies, budgetary allocations are treated as a measure of policy. This usage of the term is certainly arguable, but it is also important not to lose sight of what is distinctive about the assumption of authorized choice. When the punishment of school children ceases to be governed solely by professional judgement and comes to be governed by an explicitly stated 'discipline policy', there has been a significant change in the structuring of action.

Policy is concerned with creating coherence in the face of continuing ambiguity and contest

The problem we have been grappling with is that the map seems to be clearer than the terrain to which it relates: there is a shared image of a clear process of decision-making, but the experience is of contest, ambiguity and confusion. We have seen that policy operates on two dimensions, the vertical and the horizontal, and that this is a source of ambiguity and conflict. We have also seen that much policy activity is in response to this diffusion of organization and understanding: how do we generate concerted action when there is no single answer and little prospect of imposing one solution in the face of resistance?

This means that policy is a field that will always be marked by ambiguity and structural tension. There is structural tension between the horizontal and vertical dimensions: for instance, between having clear objectives and incorporating all the relevant participants. And there will be ambiguity arising from the different perspectives that the participants have, from the (often deliberately) imprecise language used to express them, and from the gap between the experience of the participant and the terms used to describe it.

This is the source of the frustration which analysts of policy often feel, but it is also the source of the interest. It is because there are no fixed points that participants attempt to find a point of anchorage – which is what they mean by policy. And it is the source of the rhetorical devices which the participants use to reconcile their experience with the model, such as the coexistence of 'sacred' and 'profane' accounts of the same policy experience.

Policy is problematic and graduated rather than definitive and absolute

We come to the realization that to ask, 'What is the policy on x?' is to ask the wrong question, because it does not necessarily tell us the significance of the policy (if there is one). What we want to know is, 'What determines how things are done?', and this means that we want the answers to a lot of other questions. If there is a policy, who enunciated it? What sort of people take notice of it, and in what contexts? Is it linked to the pattern of resource allocation? What other factors are at work? In what way, then, is the policy statement significant? The focus shifts from 'Is there a policy, and if so, what is it?' to, 'In what sense is there policy, and what impact does it have?' The term is not a scientific absolute, but a socially constructed variable. Policy is a concept which we use to make sense of the world – but we have to work at it.

Bibliography

Aldrich, H. E., Fowler, S. W., Liou, N. and Marsh, S. J. (1994) 'Other people's concepts: why and how we sustain historical continuity in our field', *Organization*, **1**, 65–80.

Allison, G. T. (1971) *Essence of Decision*. Boston: Little, Brown.

Anderson, J. E., Brady, D. W., Bullock, C. S. III and Stewart, J. S. Jr. (1984) *Public Policy and Politics in America*. Montgomery, CA: Brooks-Cole.

Atkinson, M. M. and Coleman, W. D. (1992) 'Policy communities, policy networks and the problems of governance', *Governance*, **5**, 154–80.

Bardach, E. (1977) *The Implementation Game*. Cambridge, MA: MIT Press.

Barrett, S. and Fudge, C. (1981) *Politics and Action*. London: Methuen.

Benveniste, G. (1973) *The Politics of Expertise*. London: Croom Helm.

Braybrooke, D. and Lindblom, C. E. (1963) *A Strategy of Decision*. New York: Free Press.

Caiden, G. E. (1982) *Public Administration*, 2nd edn. Pacific Palisades, CA: Palisades Publishers.

Castles, F. G. (1991) *On Sickness Days and Social Policy*. Sydney: Public Sector Research Centre, University of NSW.

Colebatch, H. K. and Degeling, P. (1986) 'Talking and doing in the work of administration', *Public Administration and Development*, **6**, 339–56.

Coleman, W. D. and Skogstad, G. (1990) 'Policy communities and policy networks: a structural approach', in W. D. Coleman and G. Skogstad (eds) *Policy Communities and Public Policy in Canada*. Mississauga: Copp Clark Pitman.

Considine, M. (1994) *Public Policy: A Critical Approach*. Melbourne: Macmillan.

Crossman, R. (1975) *The Diaries of a Cabinet Minister*. London: Hamilton Cape.

Cuthbertson, G. M. (1975) *Political Myth and Epic*. East Lansing, MI: Michigan State University Press.

Davies, A. F. (1964) *Australian Democracy*, 2nd edn. Melbourne: Longman.

Davis, G., Wanna, J., Warhurst, J. and Weller, P. (1993) *Public Policy in Australia*. Sydney: Allen and Unwin.

Dearlove, J. (1973) *The Politics of Policy in Local Government*. Cambridge: Cambridge University Press.

Dowding, K. (1995) 'Model or metaphor: a critical review of the policy network approach', *Political Studies*, **43**: 136–58.

Dye, T. R. (1981) *Understanding Public Policy*, 4th edn. Englewood Cliffs, NJ: Prentice-Hall.

Edelman, M. (1988) *Constructing the Political Spectacle*. Chicago, IL: Chicago University Press.

Farago, P. (1985) 'Regulating milk markets: corporatist arrangements in the Swiss dairy industry', in W. Streeck and P. Schmitter (eds) *Private Interest Government*. London: Sage.

Friedrich, C. J. (1963) *Man and his Government*. New York: McGraw-Hill.

Georgiou, P. (1973) 'The goal paradigm and notes towards a counter paradigm', *Administrative Science Quarterly,* **18**, 291–310.

Gortner, H. F. (1981) *Administration in the Public Sector*. New York: John Wiley.

Grant, W. (1985) 'Private organizations as agents of public policy: the case of milk marketing in Britain', in W. Streeck and P. Schmitter (eds) *Private Interest Government.* London: Sage.

Gregory, R. (1989) 'Political rationality or "incrementalism"? Charles E. Lindblom's enduring contribution to public policy making theory', *Policy and Politics*, **17**, 139–53.

Guba, E. G. and Lincoln, Y. S. (1989) *Fourth Generation Evaluation*. Newbury Park, CA: Sage.

Gunn, L. 1987 'Perspectives on public management', in J. Kooiman and K. A. Eliassen (eds) *Managing Public Organisations*. London: Sage.

Gusfield, J. R. (1981) *The Culture of Public Problems*. Chicago: University of Chicago Press.

Hale, D. (1988) 'Just what is a policy, anyway? And who's supposed to make it?', *Administration and Society*, **19**, 423–52.

Heclo, H. (1978) 'Issue networks and the executive establishment', in A. King (ed.) *The New American Political System*. Washington, DC: American Enterprise Institute.

Heidenheimer, A. J. (1986) '*Politics, policy* and *policey* as concepts in English and Continental languages: an attempt to explain divergences', *Review of Politics*, **48**, 3–30.

Hjern, B. and Porter, D. O. (1981) 'Implementation structures: a new unit of administrative analysis', *Organization Studies*, **2**, 211–27.

Hogwood, B. W. and Gunn, L. A. (1984) *Policy Analysis for the Real World*. London: Oxford University Press.

Howlett, M. and Ramesh, M. (1995) *Studying Public Policy*. Toronto: Oxford University Press.

Hughes, O. E. (1994) *Public Management and Administration*. Houndmills and London: Macmillan.

Jackson, R. J. (1995) 'Foreign models and Aussie rules: executive–legislative relations in Australia', *Political Theory Newsletter*, **7**, 1–18.

Jenkins, W. I. (1978) *Policy Analysis*. New York: St Martin's Press.

Jenkins-Smith, H. C. (1990) *Democratic politics and policy analysis*. Pacific Grove, CA: Brooks-Cole.

Kingdon, J. W. (1984) *Agendas, Alternatives and Public Policies*. Boston, MA: Little, Brown.

Koyanagi, C. (1994) 'Is there a national policy for children and youth with serious emotional disturbance?' *Policy Studies Journal*, **22**, 669–80.

Laffin, M. (1986) *Professionalism and Policy*. Aldershot: Gower.

Lasswell, H. D. (1936) *Politics: Who Gets What, When and How*. Cleveland, OH: Meridian Books.

Lasswell, H. D. (1951) 'The policy orientation', in D. Lerner and H. D. Lasswell (eds) *The Policy Sciences*. Stanford, CA: Stanford University Press.

Lasswell, H. D. and Kaplan, A. (1970) *Power and Society*. New Haven: Yale University Press.

Laumann, E. O. and Knoke, D. (1987) *The Organizational State*. Madison: University of Wisconsin Press.

Lindblom, C. E. (1959) 'The science of muddling through', *Public Administration Review*, **19**, 78–88.

Lindblom, C. E. (1965) *The Intelligence of Democracy*. New York: Free Press.

Lindblom, C. E. (1979) 'Still muddling, not yet through', *Public Administration Review*, **39**, 517–26.

Lindblom, C. E. and Woodhouse, E. J. (1993) *The Policy-making Process*. Englewood Cliffs, NJ: Prentice-Hall.

Linder, S. H. and Peters, B. G. (1987) 'A design perspective on policy implementation: the fallacies of misplaced prescription', *Policy Studies Review*, **6**, 459–75.

March, J. G. and Olsen, J. P. (1989) *Rediscovering Institutions*. New York: Free Press.

Marsh, D. and Rhodes, R. A. W. (eds) (1992) *Policy Networks in British Government*. Oxford: Clarendon Press.

May, J. V. and Wildavsky, A. (eds) (1978) *The Policy Cycle*. Beverly Hills, CA: Sage.

Meltsner, A. J. (1976) *Policy Analysts in the Bureaucracy*. Berkeley, CA: University of California Press.

Metcalfe, L. and Richards, S. (1992) *Improving Public Management*. London: Sage.

Mintzberg, H. (1971) 'Managerial work: analysis from observation', *Management Science*, **October**, B97–B110.

Osborne, B. and Gaebler, T. (1992) *Reinventing Government*. Reading, MA: Addison-Wesley.

Ostrom, V. and Sabetti, P. (1975) 'Theory of public policy', in S. S. Nagel (ed.) *Policy Studies in America and Elsewhere*. Lexington, MA: Lexington Books.

Painter, M. (1981) 'The coordination of urban policies: land use and transportation in North Sydney, 1970–5', in S. Encel and P. Wilenski (eds) *Decisions*. Melbourne: Longman Cheshire.

Painter, M. and Carey, B. (1979) *Politics Between Departments*. St Lucia: University of Queensland Press.

Palumbo, D. J. and Calista, D. J. (1990) *Implementation and the Policy Process: Opening Up the Black Box*. New York: Greenwood Press.

Parker, R. S. (1960) 'Policy and administration', *Public Administration (Sydney)*, **19**, 113–20.

Parsons, W. (1995) *Public Policy: an introduction to the theory and practice of policy analysis*. Aldershot: Edward Elgar.

Perrow, C. (1986) *Complex Organizations*. New York: Random House.

Powell, W. W. and DiMaggio, P. J. (1991) *The New Institutionalism in Organizational Analysis*. Chicago: University of Chicago Press.

Pressman, J. and Wildavsky, A. (1973) *Implementation*. Berkeley: University of California Press.

Pressman, J. and Wildavsky, A. (1979) *Implementation*, 2nd edn. Berkeley: University of California Press.

Pressman, J. and Wildavsky, A. (1983) *Implementation*, 3rd edn. Berkeley: University of California Press.

Rhodes, R. A. W. (ed.) (1992) *Policy Networks in British Government*. Oxford: Oxford University Press.

Richardson, J. J. and Jordan, A. G. (1979) *Governing Under Pressure*. Oxford: Martin Robertson.

Ripley, R. and Franklin, G. (1984) *Congress, the Bureaucracy and Public Policy*, 2nd edn. Homewood: Dorsey.

Rossi, P. H. and Freeman, H. (1993) *Evaluation: A Systematic Approach*. Newbury Park, CA: Sage.

Sabatier, P. A. (1986) 'Top-down and bottom-up approaches to implementation research: a critical analysis and suggested synthesis', *Journal of Public Policy*, **6**, 21–48.

Sabatier, P. A. and Jenkins-Smith, H. C. (1993) *Policy Change and Learning: An Advocacy Coalition Approach*. Boulder, CO: Westview Press.

Sabatier, P. A. and Mazmanian, D. (1979) 'The conditions of effective implementation: a guide to achieving policy objectives', *Policy Analysis*, **5**, 481–504.

Schaffer, B. B. (1973) 'Policy decisions and institutional evaluation', *Development and Change*, 5, 20–47.

Schaffer, B. B. (1977) 'On the politics of policy', *Australian Journal of Politics and History*, 23, 146–55.

Schaffer, B. B. and Corbett, D. C. (1965) *Decisions*. Melbourne: Cheshire.

Schmidt, M. R. (1993) 'Grout: Alternative kinds of knowledge and why they are ignored', *Public Administration Review*, 53, 525–30.

Schön, M. and Rein, M. (1994) *Frame Reflection*. New York: Basic Books.

Scott, W. R. and Meyer, J. (1991) 'The organization of societal sectors: propositions and early evidence', in W. W. Powell and P. J. DiMaggio (eds) *The New Institutionalism in Organizational Analysis*. Chicago: University of Chicago Press.

Self, P. (1975) *Econocrats and the Policy Process*. London: Macmillan.

Smith, G. and May, D. (1980) 'The artificial debate between rationalist and incrementalist models of decision-making', *Policy and Politics*, 8, 147–61.

Stone, D. A. (1988) *Policy Paradox and Political Reason*. Glenview, IL: Scott, Foresman and Co.

Streeck, W. and Schmitter, P. (eds) (1985) *Private Interest Government*. London: Sage.

Taylor, S. (1984) *Making Bureaucracies Think*. Stanford, CA: Stanford University Press.

Truman, D. (1971) *The Governmental Process*, 2nd edn. NY: Knopf.

Uhr, J. and Mackay, K. (1992) 'Trends in program evaluation: guest editors' introduction', *Australian Journal of Public Administration*, 51, 433–5.

van Waarden, F. (1985) 'Varieties of collective self-regulation of business: the example of the Dutch dairy industry', in W. Streeck and P. Schmitter (eds) *Private Interest Government*. London: Sage.

van Waarden, F. and Schmitter, P. (eds) (1992) 'Dimensions and types of policy networks', *European Journal of Political Research*, 21: 29–52.

Walter, J. (1986) *The Minister's Minders: Personal Advisers in National Government*. Melbourne: Oxford University Press.

Wamsley, G. L. *et al.* (1990) *Refounding Public Administration*. Newbury Park, MA: Sage.

Weick, K. E. (1979) *The Social Psychology of Organizing*, 2nd edn. Reading, MA: Addison-Wesley.

Wilson, W. (1887) 'The study of administration', *Political Science Quarterly*, 2, 197–222.

Yanow, D. (1996) *How Does a Policy Mean?* Washington: Georgetown University Press.

Index